A Prentice Hall Pocket Reader

SOCIOLOGICAL CLASSICS

Edited by
David Kauzlarich
Southern Illinois University—Edwardsville

PEARSON
Prentice Hall

Upper Saddle River, New Jersey 07458

PEARSON
Prentice
Hall

Upper Saddle River, New Jersey 07458

10 9 8 7 6

ISBN 0-13-191806-0

Printed in the United States of America

CONTENTS

Preface v

1. *The Promise of Sociology* 1
   C. Wright Mills

2. *Invitation to Sociology* 9
   Peter L. Berger

3. *The Social Construction of Reality* 17
   Peter L. Berger and Thomas Luckmann

4. *Manifesto of the Communist Party* 28
   Karl Marx and Friedrich Engels

5. *The Protestant Ethic and the Spirit of Capitalism* 38
   Max Weber

6. *The Division of Labor in Society* 48
   Emile Durkheim

7. *The Souls of Black Folk* 59
   W.E.B. Du Bois

8. *Society in America* 65
   Harriet Martineau

9. *If Men Were Seeking the Franchise* 73
   Jane Addams

10. *Manifest and Latent Functions* 77
    Robert K. Merton

11. *Self and Society* 88
    George Herbert Mead

12. *The Presentation of Self in Everyday Life* 98
    Erving Goffman

13. *Body Ritual among the Nacirema* 110
    Horace Miner

14. *The Two Marriages* 115
    Jessie Bernard

15. *The Power Elite* 124
    C. Wright Mills

Acknowledgments 133

PREFACE

Sociology is a dynamic and diverse academic discipline. A good deal of this variety stems from the nature of society itself, as social life in relation to social structure, culture, and interaction is both ubiquitous and complex. The wide purview of sociology is accompanied by a range of theoretical and methodological approaches that sociologists use to understand society. Even a cursory glance at any introductory sociology textbook reveals the immense variety of topics and perspectives within the discipline. Topics covered in such books usually include: sociological theories, methods, gender, sexuality, race, ethnicity, the workplace, organizations, deviance and crime, politics, economics, marriage and family, education, globalization, religion, health, health care, population, aging, urbanization, social movements, and the natural environment. Sociology extends into even more areas. Consider that the major U.S. academic sociology organization—the American Sociological Association—contains over forty sections, each representing a different area of sociological inquiry. These areas include Aging and the Life Course; Alcohol and Drugs; Animals and Society; Asia and Asian America; Children and Youth; Collective Behavior and Social Movements; Communication and Information Technologies; Community and Urban Sociology; Comparative and Historical Sociology; Crime, Law, and Deviance; Economic Sociology; Environment and Technology; Family; History of Sociology; International Migration; Labor and Labor Movements; Latino/a Sociology; Marxist Sociology; Mathematical Sociology; Medical Sociology; Methodology; Organizations; Occupations and Work; Peace, War, and Social Conflict; Political Sociology; Political Economy of the World Systems; Race, Gender, and Class; Racial and Ethnic Minorities; Rationality and Society; Science, Knowledge, and Technology; Sex and Gender; Social Psychology; Sociological Practice; Sociology of Culture; Sociology of Education; Sociology of Emotions; Sociology of Law; Sociology of Mental Health; Sociology of Population; Sociology of Religion; Sociology of Sexualities; Teaching and Learning; and Theory. As you can see, sociology is highly applicable to our everyday lives and the larger social environment in which we which live.

The two main criteria used to select the contributions in this reader were their importance to the discipline and their illustrative potential for the beginning sociology student. All of the works included here have made a substantial impact on the development and growth of the study of society. While the intelligibility of the readings to the average undergraduate sociology student is an open question, I have edited the contributions with an eye toward their potential pedagogical utility. Some of the editorial decisions were difficult, as sometimes good, but not quite crucial portions of text have been omitted. I hope readers find that my shaping of the texts provides an authentic representation of the spirit and substance of the authors' work, and proves to be effective in helping students get the most from their reading. To further enhance classroom use, I have provided a brief introduction to each selection.

Various sociological approaches are represented in this collection. Classical sociology, like other disciplines and much of society, was almost entirely controlled by white men at the exclusion of all other groups. But it is becoming more apparent that, while marginalized at the time and to some extent today, thinkers such as Harriet Martineau, Jane Addams, and W.E.B. Du Bois were powerful molders of the sociological perspective. In addition to having some diversity in this way, this reader also includes a good variety of pieces from different sociological perspectives, as there are selections from three of the major sociological traditions: conflict, functionalist, and interactionism. For example, selections from the groundbreaking works of Marx, Weber, Durkheim, and Mead are included along with some of their outgrowths, as represented in the writings of Mills, Berger, Luckmann, and Goffman.

Early sociologists struggled to make sense out of the social world. Contemporary sociologists do the same, but with close to a century and a half of work upon which to pursue their understanding of society. We can learn much about present day affairs in society by grappling with, through, and beyond the classics like those presented here.

Finally, I would like to acknowledge the support for this project given to me by my colleagues at Southern Illinois University Edwardsville. In particular, I would like to extend my appreciation to John E. Farley, Linda Markowitz, and Connie Frey for providing me with helpful feedback. Any errors, of course, are mine alone.

David Kauzlarich

Southern Illinois University Edwardsville

C. Wright Mills (1916–1962) is one of the most familiar sociologists of the twentieth century, as he has contributed greatly to the study of politics, economics, and sociological theory. In his explication of the sociological imagination, Mills asserts that sociology encourages us to see individuals as shaped by larger historical forces and social structures. At the heart of the sociological imagination is the ability to distinguish between "troubles," which are immediate to the individual, and "issues," which are environmental, as they are situated at the institutional level of society.

THE PROMISE OF SOCIOLOGY

C. Wright Mills

Nowadays men often feel that their private lives are a series of traps. They sense that within their everyday worlds, they cannot overcome their troubles, and in this feeling, they are often quite correct: What ordinary men are directly aware of and what they try to do are bounded by the private orbits in which they live; their visions and their powers are limited to the close-up scenes of job, family, neighborhood; in other milieux, they move vicariously and remain spectators. And the more aware they become, however vaguely, of ambitions and of threats which transcend their immediate locales, the more trapped they seem to feel.

Underlying this sense of being trapped are seemingly impersonal changes in the very structure of continent-wide societies. The facts of contemporary history are also facts about the success and the failure of individual men and women. When a society is industrialized, a peasant becomes a worker; a feudal lord is liquidated or becomes a businessman. When classes rise or fall, a man is employed or unemployed; when the rate of investment goes up or down, a man takes new heart or goes broke. When wars happen, an insurance salesman becomes a rocket launcher; a store clerk, a radar man; a wife lives alone; a child grows up without a father. Neither the life of an individual nor the history of a society can be understood without understanding both.

Yet men do not usually define the troubles they endure in terms of historical change and institutional contradiction. The well-being they enjoy, they do not usually impute to the big ups and downs of the societies in which they live. Seldom aware of the intricate connection between the patterns of their own lives and the course of world history, ordinary men do not usually know what this connection means for the kinds of men they are becoming and for the kinds of history-making in which they might take part. They do not possess the quality of mind essential to grasp the interplay of man and society, of biography and history, of self and world. They cannot cope with their personal troubles in such ways as to control the structural transformations that usually lie behind them.

Surely it is no wonder. In what period have so many men been so totally exposed at so fast a pace to such earthquakes of change? That Americans have not known such catastrophic changes as have the men and women of other societies is due to historical facts that are now quickly becoming 'merely history.' The history that now affects every man is world history. Within this scene and this period, in the course of a single generation, one sixth of mankind is transformed from all that is feudal and backward into all that is modern, advanced, and fearful. Political colonies are freed; new and less visible forms of imperialism installed. Revolutions occur; men feel the intimate grip of new kinds of authority. Totalitarian societies rise, and are smashed to bits—or succeed fabulously. After two centuries of ascendancy, capitalism is shown up as only one way to make society into an industrial apparatus. After two centuries of hope, even formal democracy is restricted to a quite small portion of mankind. Everywhere in the underdeveloped world, ancient ways of life are broken up and vague expectations become urgent demands. Everywhere in the overdeveloped world, the means of authority and of violence become total in scope and bureaucratic in form. Humanity itself now lies before us, the super-nation at either pole concentrating its most co-ordinated and massive efforts upon the preparation of World War Three.

The very shaping of history now outpaces the ability of men to orient themselves in accordance with cherished values. And which values? Even when they do not panic, men often sense that older ways of feeling and thinking have collapsed and that newer beginnings are ambiguous to the point of moral stasis. Is it any wonder that ordinary men feel they cannot cope with the larger worlds with which they are so suddenly confronted? That they cannot understand the meaning of their epoch for their own lives? That—in defense of selfhood—they become morally insensible, trying to remain altogether private men? Is it any wonder that they come to be possessed by a sense of the trap?

It is not only information that they need—in this Age of Fact, information often dominates their attention and overwhelms their capacities to assimilate it. It is not only the skills of reason that they need—although their struggles to acquire these often exhaust their limited moral energy.

What they need, and what they feel they need, is a quality of mind that will help them to use information and to develop reason in order to achieve lucid summations of what is going on in the world and of what may be happening within themselves. It is this quality, I am going to contend, that journalists and scholars, artists and publics, scientists and editors are coming to expect of what may be called the sociological imagination.

1

The sociological imagination enables its possessor to understand the larger historical scene in terms of its meaning for the inner life and the external career of a variety of individuals. It enables him to take into account how individuals, in the welter of their daily experience, often become falsely conscious of their social positions. Within that welter, the framework of modern society is sought, and within that framework the psychologies of a variety of men and women are formulated. By such means the personal uneasiness of individuals is focused upon explicit troubles and the indifference of publics is transformed into involvement with public issues.

The first fruit of this imagination—and the first lesson of the social science that embodies it—is the idea that the individual can understand his own experience and gauge his own fate only by locating himself within his period, that he can know his own chances in life only by becoming aware of those of all individuals in his circumstances. In many ways it is a terrible lesson; in many ways a magnificent one. We do not know the limits of man's capacities for supreme effort or willing degradation, for agony or glee, for pleasurable brutality or the sweetness of reason. But in our time we have come to know that the limits of 'human nature' are frighteningly broad. We have come to know that every individual lives, from one generation to the next, in some society; that he lives out a biography, and that he lives it out within some historical sequence. By the fact of his living he contributes, however minutely, to the shaping of this society and to the course of its history, even as he is made by society and by its historical push and shove.

The sociological imagination enables us to grasp history and biography and the relations between the two within society. That is its task and its promise. To recognize this task and this promise is the mark of the classic social analyst. It is characteristic of Herbert Spencer—turgid, polysyllabic, comprehensive; of E. A. Ross—graceful, muckraking, upright; of Auguste Comte and Emile Durkheim; of the intricate and subtle Karl Mannheim. It is the quality of all that is intellectually excellent in Karl Marx; it is the clue to Thorstein Veblen's brilliant and ironic insight, to Joseph Schumpeter's many-sided constructions of reality; it is the basis of the psychological sweep of W. E. H. Lecky no less than of the profundity and clarity of Max Weber. And it is the signal of what is best in contemporary studies of man and society.

No social study that does not come back to the problems of biography, of history and of their intersections within a society has completed its intellectual journey. Whatever the specific problems of the classic social analysts, however limited or however broad the features of social reality they have examined, those who have been imaginatively aware of the promise of their work have consistently asked three sorts of questions:

(1) What is the structure of this particular society as a whole? What are its essential components, and how are they related to one another? How does it differ from other varieties of social order? Within it, what is the meaning of any particular feature for its continuance and for its change?
(2) Where does this society stand in human history? What are the mechanics by which it is changing? What is its place within and its meaning for the development of humanity as a whole? How does any particular feature we are examining affect, and how is it affected by, the historical period in which it moves? And this period—what are its essential features? How does it differ from other periods? What are its characteristic ways of history-making?
(3) What varieties of men and women now prevail in this society and in this period? And what varieties are coming to prevail? In what ways are

they selected and formed, liberated and repressed, made sensitive and blunted? What kinds of 'human nature' are revealed in the conduct and character we observe in this society in this period? And what is the meaning for 'human nature' of each and every feature of the society we are examining?

Whether the point of interest is a great power state or a minor literary mood, a family, a prison, a creed—these are the kinds of questions the best social analysts have asked. They are the intellectual pivots of classic studies of man in society—and they are the questions inevitably raised by any mind possessing the sociological imagination. For that imagination is the capacity to shift from one perspective to another—from the political to the psychological; from examination of a single family to comparative assessment of the national budgets of the world; from the theological school to the military establishment; from considerations of an oil industry to studies of contemporary poetry. It is the capacity to range from the most impersonal and remote transformations to the most intimate features of the human self—and to see the relations between the two. Back of its use there is always the urge to know the social and historical meaning of the individual in the society and in the period in which he has his quality and his being.

That, in brief, is why it is by means of the sociological imagination that men now hope to grasp what is going on in the world, and to understand what is happening in themselves as minute points of the intersections of biography and history within society. In large part, contemporary man's self-conscious view of himself as at least an outsider, if not a permanent stranger, rests upon an absorbed realization of social relativity and of the transformative power of history. The sociological imagination is the most fruitful form of this self-consciousness. By its use men whose mentalities have swept only a series of limited orbits often come to feel as if suddenly awakened in a house with which they had only supposed themselves to be familiar. Correctly or incorrectly, they often come to feel that they can now provide themselves with adequate summations, cohesive assessments, comprehensive orientations. Older decisions that once appeared sound now seem to them products of a mind unaccountably dense. Their capacity for astonishment is made lively again. They acquire a new way of thinking, they experience a transvaluation of values: in a word, by their reflection and by their sensibility, they realize the cultural meaning of the social sciences.

2

Perhaps the most fruitful distinction with which the sociological imagination works is between 'the personal troubles of milieu' and 'the public issues of social structure.' This distinction is an essential tool of the sociological imagination and a feature of all classic work in social science.

Troubles occur within the character of the individual and within the range of his immediate relations with others; they have to do with his self and with those limited areas of social life of which he is directly and personally aware.

Accordingly, the statement and the resolution of troubles properly lie within the individual as a biographical entity and within the scope of his immediate milieu—the social setting that is directly open to his personal experience and to some extent his willful activity. A trouble is a private matter: values cherished by an individual are felt by him to be threatened.

Issues have to do with matters that transcend these local environments of the individual and the range of his inner life. They have to do with the organization of many such milieux into the institutions of an historical society as a whole, with the ways in which various milieux overlap and interpenetrate to form the larger structure of social and historical life. An issue is a public matter: some value cherished by publics is felt to be threatened. Often there is a debate about what that value really is and about what it is that really threatens it. This debate is often without focus if only because it is the very nature of an issue, unlike even widespread trouble, that it cannot very well be defined in terms of the immediate and everyday environments of ordinary men. An issue, in fact, often involves a crisis in institutional arrangements, and often too it involves what Marxists call 'contradictions' or 'antagonisms.'

In these terms, consider unemployment. When, in a city of 100,000, only one man is unemployed, that is his personal trouble, and for its relief we properly look to the character of the man, his skills, and his immediate opportunities. But when in a nation of 50 million employees, 15 million men are unemployed, that is an issue, and we may not hope to find its solution within the range of opportunities open to any one individual. The very structure of opportunities has collapsed. Both the correct statement of the problem and the range of possible solutions require us to consider the economic and political institutions of the society, and not merely the personal situation and character of a scatter of individuals.

Consider war. The personal problem of war, when it occurs, may be how to survive it or how to die in it with honor; how to make money out of it; how to climb into the higher safety of the military apparatus; or how to contribute to the war's termination. In short, according to one's values, to find a set of milieux and within it to survive the war or make one's death in it meaningful. But the structural issues of war have to do with its causes; with what types of men it throws up into command; with its effects upon economic and political, family and religious institutions, with the unorganized irresponsibility of a world of nation-states.

Consider marriage. Inside a marriage a man and a woman may experience personal troubles, but when the divorce rate during the first four years of marriage is 250 out of every 1,000 attempts, this is an indication of a structural issue having to do with the institutions of marriage and the family and other institutions that bear upon them.

Or consider the metropolis—the horrible, beautiful, ugly, magnificent sprawl of the great city. For many upper-class people, the personal solution to 'the problem of the city' is to have an apartment with private garage under it in the heart of the city, and forty miles out, a house by Henry Hill, garden by Garrett Eckbo, on a hundred acres of private land. In these two controlled environments—with a small staff at each end and a private helicopter connection—most people could solve many of the problems of personal milieux caused by the facts of the city. But all this, however splendid, does not solve the public issues that the structural fact of the city poses. What should be done with this wonderful monstrosity? Break it all up into scattered units, combining residence and work? Refurbish it as it stands? Or, after evacuation, dynamite it and build new cities according to new plans in new places? What should those plans be? And who is to decide and to accomplish whatever choice is made? These are structural issues; to confront them and to solve them requires us to consider political and economic issues that affect innumerable milieux.

In so far as an economy is so arranged that slumps occur, the problem of unemployment becomes incapable of personal solution. In so far as war is inherent in the nation-state system and in the uneven industrialization of the world, the ordinary individual in his restricted milieu will be powerless—with or without psychiatric aid—to solve the troubles this system or lack of system imposes upon him. In so far as the family as an institution turns women into darling little slaves and men into their chief providers and unweaned dependents, the problem of a satisfactory marriage remains incapable of purely private solution. In so far as the overdeveloped megalopolis and the overdeveloped automobile are built-in features of the overdeveloped society, the issues of urban living will not be solved by personal ingenuity and private wealth.

What we experience in various and specific milieux, I have noted, is often caused by structural changes. Accordingly, to understand the changes of many personal milieux we are required to look beyond them. And the number and variety of such structural changes increase as the institutions within which we live become more embracing and more intricately connected with one another. To be aware of the idea of social structure and to use it with sensibility is to be capable of tracing such linkages among a great variety of milieux. To be able to do that is to possess the sociological imagination.

3

What are the major issues for publics and the key troubles of private individuals in our time? To formulate issues and troubles, we must ask what values are cherished, yet threatened, and what values are cherished and supported, by the characterizing trends of our period. In the case both of threat and of support we must ask what salient contradictions of structure may be involved.

When people cherish some set of values and do not feel any threat to them, they experience *well-being*. When they cherish values but *do* feel them to be threatened, they experience a crisis—either as a personal trouble or as a public issue. And if all their values seem involved, they feel the total threat of panic.

But suppose people are neither aware of any cherished values nor experience any threat? That is the experience of *indifference*, which, if it seems to involve all their values, becomes apathy. Suppose, finally, they are unaware of any cherished values, but still are very much aware of a threat? That is the experience of *uneasiness*, of anxiety, which, if it is total enough, becomes a deadly unspecified malaise.

Ours is a time of uneasiness and indifference—not yet formulated in such ways as to permit the work of reason and the play of sensibility. Instead of troubles—defined in terms of values and threats—there is often the misery of vague uneasiness; instead of explicit issues there is often merely the beat feeling that all is somehow not right. Neither the values threatened nor whatever threatens them has been stated; in short, they have not been carried to the point of decision. Much less have they been formulated as problems of social science.

In the 'thirties there was little doubt—except among certain deluded business circles that there was an economic issue which was also a pack of personal troubles. In these arguments about 'the crisis of capitalism,' the formulations of Marx and the many unacknowledged re-formulations of his work probably set the leading terms of the issue, and some men came to understand their personal troubles in these terms. The values threatened were plain to see and cherished by all; the structural contradictions that threatened them also seemed plain. Both were widely and deeply experienced. It was a political age.

But the values threatened in the era after World War Two are often neither widely acknowledged as values nor widely felt to be threatened. Much private uneasiness goes unformulated; much public malaise and many decisions of enormous structural relevance never become public issues. For those who accept such inherited values as reason and freedom, it is the uneasiness itself that is the trouble; it is the indifference itself that is the issue. And it is this condition, of uneasiness and indifference, that is the signal feature of our period.

All this is so striking that it is often interpreted by observers as a shift in the very kinds of problems that need now to be formulated. We are frequently told that the problems of our decade, or even the crises of our period, have shifted from the external realm of economics and now have to do with the quality of individual life—in fact with the question of whether there is soon going to be anything that can properly be called individual life. Not child labor but comic books, not poverty but mass leisure, are at the center of concern. Many great public issues as well as many private troubles are described in terms of 'the psychiatric'—often, it seems, in a pathetic attempt to avoid the large issues and problems of modern society. Often this statement seems to rest upon a provincial narrowing of interest to the Western societies, or even to the United States—thus ignoring two-thirds of mankind; often, too, it arbitrarily divorces the individual life from the larger institutions within which that life is enacted, and which on occasion bear upon it more grievously than do the intimate environments of childhood.

Problems of leisure, for example, cannot even be stated without considering problems of work. Family troubles over comic books cannot be formulated as problems without considering the plight of the contemporary family in its new relations with the newer institutions of the social structure. Neither leisure nor its debilitating uses can be understood as problems without recognition of the extent to which malaise and indifference now form the social and personal climate of contemporary American society. In this climate, no problems of 'the private life' can be stated and solved without recognition of the crisis of ambition that is part of the very career of men at work in the incorporated economy.

It is true, as psychoanalysts continually point out, that people do often have 'the increasing sense of being moved by obscure forces within themselves which they are unable to define.' But it is *not* true, as Ernest Jones asserted, that 'man's chief enemy and danger is his own unruly nature and the dark forces pent up within him.' On the contrary: 'Man's chief danger' today lies in the unruly forces of contemporary society itself, with its alienating methods of production, its enveloping techniques of political domination, its international anarchy—in a word, its pervasive transformations of the very 'nature' of man and the conditions and aims of his life.

It is now the social scientist's foremost political and intellectual task—for here the two coincide—to make clear the elements of contemporary uneasiness and indifference. It is the central demand made upon him by other cultural workmen—by physical scientists and artists, by the intellectual community in general. It is because of this task and these demands, I believe, that the social sciences are becoming the common denominator of our cultural period, and the sociological imagination our most needed quality of mind.

In this selection, Peter L. Berger provides us with an invitation to sociology by detailing how the sociological approach differs from that of conventional wisdom and standpoints characteristic of other academic disciplines, such as economics and law. Berger also discusses how the terms "society," "social," and "social problems" are conceptualized by sociologists. Sociology, he explains, acknowledges that there are multiple levels of reality. This provides one with the ability to see behind and through social structure.

INVITATION TO SOCIOLOGY

Peter L. Berger

The peculiarity of sociological perspective becomes clear with some reflection concerning the meaning of the term "society," a term that refers to the object *par excellence* of the discipline. Like most terms used by sociologists, this one is derived from common usage, where its meaning is imprecise. Sometimes it means a particular band of people (as in "Society for the Prevention of Cruelty to Animals"), sometimes only those people endowed with great prestige or privilege (as in "Boston society ladies"), and on other occasions it is simply used to denote company of any sort (for example, "he greatly suffered in those years for lack of society"). There are other, less frequent meanings as well. The sociologist uses the term in a more precise sense, though, of course, there are differences in usage within the discipline itself. The sociologist thinks of "society" as denoting a large complex of human relationships, or to put it in more technical language, as referring to a system of interaction. The word "large" is difficult to specify quantitatively in this context. The sociologist may speak of a "society" including millions of human beings (say, "American society"), but he may also use the term to refer to a numerically much smaller collectivity (say, "the society of sophomores on this campus"). Two people chatting on a street corner will hardly constitute a "society," but three people stranded on an island certainly will. The applicability of the concept, then, cannot be decided on quantitative grounds alone. It rather applies when a complex of relationships is sufficiently succinct to be analyzed by itself, understood as an autonomous entity, set against others of the same kind.

The adjective "social" must be similarly sharpened for sociological use. In common speech it may denote, once more, a number of different things—the informal quality of a certain gathering ("this is a social meeting—let's not discuss business"), an altruistic attitude on somebody's part ("he had a strong social concern in his job"), or, more generally, anything derived from contact with other people ("a social disease"). The sociologist will use the term more narrowly and more precisely to refer to the quality of interaction, interrelationship, mutuality. Thus two men chatting on a street corner do not constitute a "society," but what transpires between them is certainly "social." "Society" consists of a complex of such "social" events. As to the exact definition of the "social," it is difficult to improve on Max Weber's definition of a "social" situation as one in which people orient their actions towards one another. The web of meanings, expectations and conduct resulting from such mutual orientation is the stuff of sociological analysis.

Yet this refinement of terminology is not enough to show up the distinctiveness of the sociological angle of vision. We may get closer by comparing the latter with the perspective of other disciplines concerned with human actions. The economist, for example, is concerned with the analyses of processes that occur in society and that can be described as social. These processes have to do with the basic problem of economic activity—the allocation of scarce goods and services within a society. The economist will be concerned with these processes in terms of the way in which they carry out, or fail to carry out, this function. The sociologist, in looking at the same processes, will naturally have to take into consideration their economic purpose. But his distinctive interest is not necessarily related to this purpose as such. He will be interested in a variety of human relationships and interactions that may occur here and that may be quite irrelevant to the economic goals in question. Thus economic activity involves relationships of power, prestige, prejudice or even play that can be analyzed with only marginal reference to the properly economic function of the activity.

The sociologist finds his subject matter present in all human activities, but not all aspects of these activities constitute this subject matter. Social interaction is not some specialized sector of what men do with each other. It is rather a certain aspect of all these doings. Another way of putting this is by saying that the sociologist carries on a special sort of abstraction. The social, as an object of inquiry, is not a segregated field of human activity. Rather (to borrow a phrase from Lutheran sacramental theology) it is present "in, with and under" many different fields of such activity. The sociologist does not look at phenomena that nobody else is aware of. But he looks at the same phenomena in a different way.

As a further example we could take the perspective of the lawyer. Here we actually find a point of view much broader in scope than that of the economist. Almost any human activity can, at one time or another, fall within the province of the lawyer. This, indeed, is the fascination of the law. Again, we find here a very special procedure of abstraction. From the immense wealth and variety of human deportment the lawyer selects those aspects that are pertinent (or, as he would say, "material") to his very particular frame of reference. As anyone who has ever been involved in a lawsuit well knows, the criteria of what is relevant or irrelevant legally will often greatly surprise the principals in the case in question. This need not concern us here. We would rather observe that the legal frame of reference consists of a number of carefully defined models of human activity. Thus we have clear models of obligation, responsibility or wrongdoing. Definite conditions have to prevail before any empirical act can be subsumed under one of these headings, and these conditions are laid down by statutes or precedent. When these conditions are not met, the act in question is legally irrelevant. The expertise of the lawyer consists of knowing the rules by which these models are constructed. He knows, within his frame of reference, when a business contract is binding, when the driver of an automobile may be held to be negligent, or when rape has taken place.

The sociologist may look at these same phenomena, but his frame of reference will be quite different. Most importantly, his perspective on these phenomena cannot be derived from statutes or precedent. His interest in the human relationships occurring in a business transaction has no bearing on the legal validity of contracts signed, just as sociologically interesting deviance in sexual behavior may not be capable of being subsumed under some particular legal heading. From the lawyer's point of view, the sociologist's inquiry is extraneous to the legal frame of reference. One might say that, with reference to the conceptual edifice of the law, the sociologist's activity is subterranean in character. The lawyer is concerned with what may be called the official conception of the situation. The sociologist often deals with very unofficial conceptions indeed. For the lawyer the essential thing to understand is how the law looks upon a certain type of criminal. For the sociologist it is equally important to see how the criminal looks at the law.

To ask sociological questions, then, presupposes that one is interested in looking some distance beyond the commonly accepted or officially defined goals of human actions. It presupposes a certain awareness that human events have different levels of meaning, some of which are hidden from the consciousness of everyday life. It may even presuppose a measure of suspicion about the way in which human events are officially interpreted by the authorities, be they political, juridical or religious in character. If one is willing to go as far as that, it would seem evident that not all historical circumstances are equally favorable for the development of sociological perspective.

It would appear plausible, in consequence, that sociological thought would have the best chance to develop in historical circumstances marked by severe jolts to the self-conception, especially the official and authoritative and generally accepted self-conception, of a culture. It is only in such circumstances that perceptive men are likely to be motivated to think beyond the assertions of this self-conception and, as a result, question the authorities. Albert Salomon has argued cogently that the concept of "society," in its modern sociological sense, could emerge only as the normative structures of Christendom and later of the *ancien régime* were collapsing. We can, then, again conceive of "society" as the hidden fabric of an edifice, the outside facade of which hides that fabric from the common view. In medieval Christendom, "society" was rendered invisible by the imposing religiopolitical facade that constituted the common world of European man. As Salomon pointed out, the more secular political facade of the absolute state performed the same function after the Reformation had broken up the unity of Christendom. It was with the disintegration of the absolute state that the underlying frame of "society" came into view—that is, a world of motives and forces that could not be understood in terms of the official interpretations of social reality. Sociological perspective can then be understood in terms of such phrases as "seeing through," "looking behind," very much as such phrases would be employed in common speech—"seeing through his game," "looking behind the scenes"—in other words, "being up on all the tricks."

We will not be far off if we see sociological thought as part of what Nietzsche called "the art of mistrust." Now, it would be a gross oversimplification to think that this art has existed only in modern times. "Seeing through" things is probably a pretty general function of intelligence, even in very primitive societies. The American anthropologist Paul Radin has provided us with a vivid description of the skeptic as a human type in primitive culture. We also have evidence from civilizations other than that of the modern West, bearing witness to forms of consciousness that could well be called protosociological. We could point, for instance, to Herodotus or to Ibn-Khaldun. There are even texts from ancient Egypt evincing a profound disenchantment with a political and social order that has acquired the reputation of having been one of the most cohesive in human history. However, with the beginning of the modern era in the West this form of consciousness intensifies, becomes concentrated and systematized, marks the thought of an increasing number of perceptive men. This is not the place to discuss in detail the prehistory of sociological thought, a discussion in which we owe very much to Salomon. Nor would we even give here an intellectual table of ancestors for sociology, showing its connections with Machiavelli, Erasmus, Bacon, seventeenth-century philosophy and eighteenth-century *belles-lettres*—this has been done elsewhere and by others much more qualified than this writer. Suffice it to stress once more that sociological thought marks the fruition of a number of intellectual developments that have a very specific location in modern Western history.

Let us return instead to the proposition that sociological perspective involves a process of "seeing through" the facades of social structures. We could think of this in terms of a common experience of people living in large cities. One of the fascinations of a large city is the immense variety of human activities taking place behind the seemingly anonymous and endlessly undifferentiated rows of houses. A person who lives in such a city will time and again experience surprise or even shock as he discovers the strange pursuits that some men engage in quite unobtrusively in houses that, from the outside, look like all the others on a certain street. Having had this experience once or twice, one will repeatedly find oneself walking down a street, perhaps late in the evening, and wondering what may be going on under the bright lights showing through a line of drawn curtains. An ordinary family engaged in pleasant talk with guests? A scene of desperation amid illness or death? Or a scene of debauched pleasures? Perhaps a strange cult or a dangerous conspiracy? The facades of the houses cannot tell us, proclaiming nothing but an architectural conformity to the tastes of some group or class that may not even inhabit the street any longer. The social mysteries lie behind the facades. The wish to penetrate to these mysteries is an analogon to sociological curiosity. In some cities that are suddenly struck by calamity this wish may be abruptly realized. Those who have experienced wartime bombings know of the sudden encounters with unsuspected (and sometimes unimaginable) fellow tenants in the air-raid shelter of one's apartment building. Or they can recollect the startling morning sight of a house hit by a bomb during the night, neatly sliced in half, the facade torn away and the previously hidden interior mercilessly revealed in the daylight. But in most cities that one may normally live in, the facades must be penetrated by one's own inquisitive intrusions. Similarly, there are historical situations in which the facades of society are violently torn apart and all but the most incurious are forced to see that there was a reality behind the facades all along. Usually this does not happen and the facades continue to confront us with seemingly rocklike permanence. The perception of the reality behind the facades then demands a considerable intellectual effort.

A few examples of the way in which sociology "looks behind" the facades of social structures might serve to make our argument clearer. Take, for instance, the political organization of a community. If one wants to find out how a modern American city is governed, it is very easy to get the official information about this subject. The city will have a charter, operating under the laws of the state. With some advice from informed individuals, one may look up various statutes that define the constitution of the city. Thus one may find out that this particular community has a city-manager form of administration, or that party affiliations do not appear on the ballot in municipal elections, or that the city government participates in a regional water district. In similar fashion, with the help of some newspaper reading, one may find out the officially recognized political problems of the community. One may read that the city plans to annex a certain suburban area, or that there has been a change in the zoning ordinances to facilitate industrial development in another area, or even that one of the members of the city council has been accused of using his office for personal gain. All such matters still occur on the, as it were, visible, official or public level of political life. However, it would be an exceedingly naive person who would believe that this kind of information gives him a rounded picture of the political reality of that community. The sociologist will want to know above all the constituency of the "informal power structure" (as it has been called by Floyd Hunter, an American sociologist interested in such studies), which is a configuration of men and their power that cannot be found in any statutes, and probably cannot be read about in the newspapers. The political scientist or the legal expert might find it very interesting to compare the city charter with the constitutions of other similar communities. The sociologist will be far more concerned with discovering the way in which powerful vested interests influence or even control the actions of officials elected under the charter. These vested interests will not be found in city hall, but rather in the executive suites of corporations that may not even be located in that community, in the private mansions of a handful of powerful men, perhaps in the offices of certain labor unions or even, in some instances, in the headquarters of criminal organizations. When the sociologist concerns himself with power, he will "look behind" the official mechanisms that are supposed to regulate power in the community. This does not necessarily mean that he will regard the official mechanisms as totally ineffective or their legal definition as totally illusionary. But at the very least he will insist that there is another level of reality to be investigated in the particular system of power. In some cases he might conclude that to look for real power in the publicly recognized places is quite delusional.

Take another example. Protestant denominations in this country differ widely in their so-called "polity," that is, the officially defined way in which the denomination is run. One may speak of an episcopal, a presbyterian or a congregational "polity" (meaning by this not the denominations called by these names, but the forms of ecclesiastical government that various denominations share—for instance, the episcopal form shared by Episcopalians and Methodists, the congregational by Congregationalists and Baptists). In nearly all cases, the "polity" of a denomination is the result of a long historical development and is based on a theological rationale over which the doctrinal experts continue to quarrel. Yet a sociologist interested in studying the government of American denominations would do well not to arrest himself too long at these official definitions. He will soon find that the real questions of power and organization have little to do with "polity" in the theological sense. He will discover that the basic form of organization in all denominations of any size is bureaucratic. The logic of administrative behavior is determined by bureaucratic processes, only very rarely by the workings of an episcopal or a congregational point of view. The sociological investigator will then quickly "see through" the mass of confusing terminology denoting officeholders in the ecclesiastical bureaucracy and correctly identify those who hold executive power, no matter whether they be called "bishops," or "stated clerks" or "synod presidents." Understanding denominational organization as belonging to the much larger species of bureaucracy, the sociologist will then be able to grasp the processes that occur in the organization, to observe the internal and external pressures brought to bear on those who are theoretically in charge. In other words, behind the facade of an "episcopal polity" the sociologist will perceive the workings of a bureaucratic apparatus that is not terribly different in the Methodist Church, an agency of the Federal government, General Motors or the United Automobile Workers.

Or take an example from economic life. The personnel manager of an industrial plant will take delight in preparing brightly colored charts that show the table of organization that is supposed to administer the production process. Every man has his place, every person in the organization knows from whom he receives his orders and to whom he must transmit them, every work team has its assigned role in the great drama of production. In reality things rarely work this way—and every good personnel manager knows this. Superimposed on the official blueprint of the organization is a much subtler, much less visible network of human groups, with their loyalties, prejudices, antipathies and (most important) codes of behavior. Industrial sociology is full of data on the operations of this informal network, which always exists in varying degrees of accommodation and conflict with the official system. Very much the same coexistence of formal and informal organization are to be found wherever large numbers of men work together or live together under a system of discipline—military organizations, prisons, hospitals, schools, going back to the mysterious leagues that children form among themselves and that their parents only rarely discern. Once more, the sociologist will seek to penetrate the smoke screen of the official versions of reality (those of the foreman, the officer, the teacher) and try to grasp the signals that come from the "underworld" (those of the worker, the enlisted man, the schoolboy).

Let us take one further example. In Western countries, and especially in America, it is assumed that men and women marry because they are in love. There is a broadly based popular mythology about the character of love as a violent, irresistible emotion that strikes where it will, a mystery that is the goal of most young people and often of the not-so-young as well. As soon as one investigates, however, which people actually marry each other, one finds that the lightning-shaft of Cupid seems to be guided rather strongly within very definite channels of class, income, education, racial and religious background. If one then investigates a little further into the behavior that is engaged in prior to marriage under the rather misleading euphemism of "courtship," one finds channels of interaction that are often rigid to the point of ritual. The suspicion begins to dawn on one that, most of the time, it is not so much the emotion of love that creates a certain kind of relationship, but that carefully predefined and often planned relationships eventually generate the desired emotion. In other words, when certain conditions are met or have been constructed, one allows oneself "to fall in love." The sociologist investigating our patterns of "courtship" and marriage soon discovers a complex web of motives related in many ways to the entire institutional structure within which an individual lives his life—class, career, economic ambition, aspirations of power and prestige. The miracle of love now begins to look somewhat synthetic. Again, this need not mean in any given instance that the sociologist will declare the romantic interpretation to be an illusion. But, once more, he will look beyond the immediately given and publicly approved interpretations. Contemplating a couple that in its turn is contemplating the moon, the sociologist need not feel constrained to deny the emotional impact of the scene thus illuminated. But he will observe the machinery that went into the construction of the scene in its nonlunar aspects—the status index of the automobile from which the contemplation occurs, the canons of taste and tactics that determine the costume of the contemplators, the many ways in which language and demeanor place them socially, thus the social location and intentionality of the entire enterprise.

It may have become clear at this point that the problems that will interest the sociologist are not necessarily what other people may call "problems." The way in which public officials and newspapers (and, alas, some college textbooks in sociology) speak about "social problems" serves to obscure this fact. People commonly speak of a "social problem" when something in society does not work the way it is supposed to according to the official interpretations. They then expect the sociologist to study the "problem" as they have defined it and perhaps even to come up with a "solution" that will take care of the matter to their own satisfaction. It is important, against this sort of expectation, to understand that a sociological problem is something quite different from a "social problem" in this sense. For example, it is naive to concentrate on crime as a "problem" because law-enforcement agencies so define it, or on divorce because that is a "problem" to the moralists of marriage. Even more clearly, the "problem" of the foreman to get his men to work more efficiently or of the line officer to get his troops to charge the enemy more enthusiastically need not be problematic at all to the sociologist (leaving out of consideration for the moment the probable fact that the sociologist asked to study such "problems" is employed by the corporation or the army). The sociological problem is always the understanding of what goes on here in terms of social interaction. Thus the sociological problem is not so much why some things "go wrong" from the viewpoint of the authorities and the management of the social scene, but how the whole system works in the first place, what are its presuppositions and by what means it is held together. The fundamental sociological problem is not crime but the law, not divorce but marriage, not racial discrimination but racially defined stratification, not revolution but government.

This point can be explicated further by an example. Take a settlement house in a lower-class slum district trying to wean away teen-agers from the publicly disapproved activities of a juvenile gang. The frame of reference within which social workers and police officers define the "problems" of this situation is constituted by the world of middle-class, respectable, publicly approved values. It is a "problem" if teen-agers drive around in stolen automobiles, and it is a "solution" if instead they will play group games in the settlement house. But if one changes the frame of reference and looks at the situation from the viewpoint of the leaders of the juvenile gang, the "problems" are defined in reverse order. It is a "problem" for the solidarity of the gang if its members are seduced away from those activities that lend prestige to the gang within its own social world, and it would be a "solution" if the social workers went way the hell back uptown where they came from. What is a "problem" to one social system is the normal routine of things to the other system, and vice versa. Loyalty and disloyalty, solidarity and deviance, are defined in contradictory terms by the representatives of the two systems. Now, the sociologist may, in terms of his own values, regard the world of middle-class respectability as more desirable and therefore want to come to the assistance of the settlement house, which is its missionary outpost *in partibus infidelium*. This, however, does not justify the identification of the director's headaches with what are "problems" sociologically. The "problems" that the sociologist will want to solve concern an understanding of the entire social situation, the values and modes of action in *both* systems, and the way in which the two systems coexist in space and time. Indeed, this very ability to look at a situation from the vantage points of competing systems of interpretation is, as we shall see more clearly later on, one of the hallmarks of sociological consciousness.

We would contend, then, that there is a debunking motif inherent in sociological consciousness. The sociologist will be driven time and again, by the very logic of his discipline, to debunk the social systems he is studying. This unmasking tendency need not necessarily be due to the sociologist's temperament or inclinations. Indeed, it may happen that the sociologist, who as an individual may be of a conciliatory disposition and quite disinclined to disturb the comfortable assumptions on which he rests his own social existence, is nevertheless compelled by what he is doing to fly in the face of what those around him take for granted. In other words, we would contend that the roots of the debunking motif in sociology are not psychological but methodological. The sociological frame of reference, with its built-in procedure of looking for levels of reality other than those given in the official interpretations of society, carries with it a logical imperative to unmask the pretensions and the propaganda by which men cloak their actions with each other. This unmasking imperative is one of the characteristics of sociology particularly at home in the temper of the modern era.

Berger and Luckmann's book *The Social Construction of Reality* is subtitled "*A Treatise in the Sociology of Knowledge.*" The following excerpt from this book represents the authors' views on how ordinary people come to define reality in their everyday life, and thus how they acquire and use knowledge to guide their behavior. The most important kind of social interaction, according to Berger and Luckmann, is that which is face-to-face with other people. Social realities—that is, what we regard as real and meaningful—are created through reciprocal, fluid, and flexible interactions on a constant basis.

The Social Construction of Reality

Peter L. Berger and Thomas Luckmann

1. The Reality of Everyday Life

Since our purpose in this treatise is a sociological analysis of the reality of everyday life, more precisely, of knowledge that guides conduct in everyday life, and we are only tangentially interested in how this reality may appear in various theoretical perspectives to intellectuals, we must begin by a clarification of that reality as it is available to the commonsense of the ordinary members of society. How that commonsense reality may be influenced by the theoretical constructions of intellectuals and other merchants of ideas is a further question. Ours is thus an enterprise that, although theoretical in character, is geared to the understanding of a reality that forms the subject matter of the empirical science of sociology, that is, the world of everyday life.

It should be evident, then, that our purpose is *not* to engage in philosophy. All the same, if the reality of everyday life is to be understood, account must be taken of its intrinsic character before we can proceed with sociological analysis proper. Everyday life presents itself as a reality interpreted by men and subjectively meaningful to them as a coherent world. As sociologists we take this reality as the object of our analyses. Within the frame of reference of sociology as an empirical science it is possible to take this reality as given, to take as data particular phenomena arising within it, without further inquiring about the foundations of this reality, which is a philosophical task. However, given the particular purpose of the present treatise, we cannot completely bypass the philosophical problem. The world of everyday life is not only taken for granted as reality by the ordinary members of society in the subjectively meaningful conduct of their lives. It is a world that originates in their thoughts and actions, and is maintained as real by these. Before turning to our main task we must, therefore, attempt to clarify the foundations of knowledge in everyday life, to wit, the objectivations of subjective processes (and meanings) by which the *inter*subjective commonsense world is constructed.

For the purpose at hand, this is a preliminary task, and we can do no more than sketch the main features of what we believe to be an adequate solution to the philosophical problem—adequate, let us hasten to add, only in the sense that it can serve as a starting point for sociological analysis. The considerations immediately following are, therefore, of the nature of philosophical prolegomena and, in themselves, presociological. The method we consider best suited to clarify the foundations of knowledge in everyday life is that of phenomenological analysis, a purely descriptive method and, as such, "empirical" but not "scientific"—as we understand the nature of the empirical sciences.[1]

The phenomenological analysis of everyday life, or rather of the subjective experience of everyday life, refrains from any causal or genetic hypotheses, as well as from assertions about the ontological status of the phenomena analyzed. It is important to remember this. Commonsense contains innumerable pre- and quasi-scientific interpretations about everyday reality, which it takes for granted. If we are to describe the reality of commonsense we must refer to these interpretations, just as we must take account of its taken-for-granted character—but we do so within phenomenological brackets.

Consciousness is always intentional; it always intends or is directed toward objects. We can never apprehend some putative substratum of consciousness as such, only consciousness of something or other. This is so regardless of whether the object of consciousness is experienced as belonging to an external physical world or apprehended as an element of an inward subjective reality. Whether I (the first person singular, here as in the following illustrations, standing for ordinary self-consciousness in everyday life) am viewing the panorama of New York City or whether I become conscious of an inner anxiety, the processes of consciousness involved are intentional in both instances. The point need not be belabored that the consciousness of the Empire State Building differs from the awareness of anxiety. A detailed phenomenological analysis would uncover the various layers of experience, and the different structures of meaning involved in, say, being bitten by a dog, remembering having been bitten by a dog, having a phobia about all dogs, and so forth. What interests us here is the common intentional character of all consciousness.

Different objects present themselves to consciousness as constituents of different spheres of reality. I recognize the fellowmen I must deal with in the course of everyday life as pertaining to a reality quite different from the disembodied figures that appear in my dreams. The two sets of objects introduce quite different tensions into my consciousness and I am attentive to them in quite different ways.

---

[1] This entire section of our treatise is based on Alfred Schutz and Thomas Luckmann, *Die Strukturen der Lebenswelt*, now being prepared for publication. In view of this, we have refrained from providing individual references to the places in Schutz's published work where the same problems are discussed. Our argument here is based on Schutz, as developed by Luckmann in the afore-mentioned work, *in toto*. The reader wishing to acquaint himself with Schutz's work published to date may consult Alfred Schutz, *Der sinnhafte Aufbau der sozialen Welt* (Vienna, Springer, 1960); *Collected Papers*, Vols. I and II. The reader interested in Schutz's adaptation of the phenomenological method to the analysis of the social world may consult especially his *Collected Papers*, Vol. I, pp 99ff., and Maurice Natanson (ed.), *Philosophy of the Social Sciences* (New York, Random House, 1963), pp. 183ff.

My consciousness, then, is capable of moving through different spheres of reality. Put differently, I am conscious of the world as consisting of multiple realities. As I move from one reality to another, I experience the transition as a kind of shock. This shock is to be understood as caused by the shift in attentiveness that the transition entails. Waking up from a dream illustrates this shift most simply.

Among the multiple realities there is one that presents itself as the reality par excellence. This is the reality of everyday life. Its privileged position entitles it to the designation of paramount reality. The tension of consciousness is highest in everyday life, that is, the latter imposes itself upon consciousness in the most massive, urgent and intense manner. It is impossible to ignore, difficult even to weaken in its imperative presence. Consequently, it forces me to be attentive to it in the fullest way. I experience everyday life in the state of being wide-awake. This wide-awake state of existing in and apprehending the reality of everyday life is taken by me to be normal and self-evident, that is, it constitutes my natural attitude.

I apprehend the reality of everyday life as an ordered reality. Its phenomena are prearranged in patterns that seem to be independent of my apprehension of them and that impose themselves upon the latter. The reality of everyday life appears already objectified, that is, constituted by an order of objects that have been designated *as* objects before my appearance on the scene. The language used in everyday life continuously provides me with the necessary objectifications and posits the order within which these make sense and within which everyday life has meaning for me. I live in a place that is geographically designated; I employ tools, from can openers to sports cars, which are designated in the technical vocabulary of my society; I live within a web of human relationships, from my chess club to the United States of America, which are also ordered by means of vocabulary. In this manner language marks the co-ordinates of my life in society and fills that life with meaningful objects.

The reality of everyday life is organized around the "here" of my body and the "now" of my present. This "here and now" is the focus of my attention to the reality of everyday life. What is "here and now" presented to me in everyday life is the *realissimum* of my consciousness. The reality of everyday life is not, however, exhausted by these immediate presences, but embraces phenomena that are not present "here and now." This means that I experience everyday life in terms of differing degrees of closeness and remoteness, both spatially and temporally. Closest to me is the zone of everyday life that is directly accessible to my bodily manipulation. This zone contains the world within my reach, the world in which I act so as to modify its reality, or the world in which I work. In this world of working my consciousness is dominated by the pragmatic motive, that is, my attention to this world is mainly determined by what I am doing, have done or plan to do in it. In this way it is *my* world par excellence. I know, of course, that the reality of everyday life contains zones that are not accessible to me in this manner. But either I have no pragmatic interest in these zones or my interest in them is indirect insofar as they may be, potentially, manipulative zones for me. Typically, my interest in the far zones is less intense and certainly less urgent. I am intensely interested in the cluster of objects involved in my daily occupation—say, the world of the garage, if I am a mechanic. I am interested, though less directly, in what goes on in the testing laboratories of the automobile industry in Detroit—I am unlikely ever to be in one of these laboratories, but the work done there will eventually affect my everyday life. I may also be interested in what goes on at Cape Kennedy or in outer space, but this interest is a matter of private, "leisuretime" choice rather than an urgent necessity of my everyday life.

The reality of everyday life further presents itself to me as an intersubjective world, a world that I share with others. This intersubjectivity sharply differentiates everyday life from other realities of which I am conscious. I am alone in the world of my dreams, but I know that the world of everyday life is as real to others as it is to myself. Indeed, I cannot exist in everyday life without continually interacting and communicating with others. I know that my natural attitude to this world corresponds to the natural attitude of others, that they also comprehend the objectifications by which this world is ordered, that they also organize this world around the "here and now" of *their* being in it and have projects for working in it. I also know, of course, that the others have a perspective on this common world that is not identical with mine. My "here" is their "there." My "now" does not fully overlap with theirs. My projects differ from and may even conflict with theirs. All the same, I know that I live with them in a common world. Most importantly, I know that there is an ongoing correspondence between *my* meanings and *their* meanings in this world, that we share a common sense about its reality. The natural attitude is the attitude of commonsense consciousness precisely because it refers to a world that is common to many men. Commonsense knowledge is the knowledge I share with others in the normal, self-evident routines of everyday life.

The reality of everyday life is taken for granted as reality. It does not require additional verification over and beyond its simple presence. It is simply *there*, as self-evident and compelling facticity. I *know* that it is real. While I am capable of engaging in doubt about its reality, I am obliged to suspend such doubt as I routinely exist in everyday life. This suspension of doubt is so firm that to abandon it, as I might want to do, say, in theoretical or religious contemplation, I have to make an extreme transition. The world of everyday life proclaims itself and, when I want to challenge the proclamation, I must engage in a deliberate, by no means easy effort. The transition from the natural attitude to the theoretical attitude of the philosopher or scientist illustrates this point. But not all aspects of this reality are equally unproblematic. Everyday life is divided into sectors that are apprehended routinely, and others that present me with problems of one kind or another. Suppose that I am an automobile mechanic who is highly knowledgeable about all American-made cars. Everything that pertains to the latter is a routine, unproblematic facet of my everyday life. But one day someone appears in the garage and asks me to repair his Volkswagen. I am now compelled to enter the problematic world of foreign-made cars. I may do so reluctantly or with professional curiosity, but in either case I am now faced with problems that I have not yet routinized. At the same time, of course, I do not leave the reality of everyday life. Indeed, the latter becomes enriched as I begin to incorporate into it the knowledge and skills required for the repair of foreign-made cars. The reality of everyday life encompasses both kinds of sectors, as long as what appears as a problem does not pertain to a different reality altogether (say, the reality of theoretical physics, or of nightmares). As long as the routines of everyday life continue without interruption they are apprehended as unproblematic.

But even the unproblematic sector of everyday reality is so only until further notice, that is, until its continuity is interrupted by the appearance of a problem. When this happens, the reality of everyday life seeks to integrate the problematic sector into what is already unproblematic. Commonsense knowledge contains a variety of instructions as to how this is to be done. For instance, the others with whom I work are unproblematic to me as long as they perform their familiar, taken-for-granted routines—say, typing away at desks next to mine in my office. They become problematic if they interrupt these routines—say, huddling together in a corner and talking in whispers. As I inquire about the meaning of this unusual activity, there is a variety of possibilities that my commonsense knowledge is capable of reintegrating into the unproblematic routines of everyday life: they may be consulting on how to fix a broken typewriter, or one of them may have some urgent instructions from the boss, and so on. On the other hand, I may find that they are discussing a union directive to go on strike, something as yet outside my experience but still well within the range of problems with which my commonsense knowledge can deal. It will deal with it, though, as a problem, rather than simply reintegrating it into the unproblematic sector of everyday life. If, however, I come to the conclusion that my colleagues have gone collectively mad, the problem that presents itself is of yet another kind. I am now faced with a problem that transcends the boundaries of the reality of everyday life and points to an altogether different reality. Indeed, my conclusion that my colleagues have gone mad implies *ipso facto* that they have gone off into a world that is no longer the common world of everyday life.

Compared to the reality of everyday life, other realities appear as finite provinces of meaning, enclaves within the paramount reality marked by circumscribed meanings and modes of experience. The paramount reality envelops them on all sides, as it were, and consciousness always returns to the paramount reality as from an excursion. This is evident from the illustrations already given, as in the reality of dreams or that of theoretical thought. Similar "commutations" take place between the world of everyday life and the world of play, both the playing of children and, even more sharply, of adults. The theater provides an excellent illustration of such playing on the part of adults. The transition between realities is marked by the rising and falling of the curtain. As the curtain rises, the spectator is "transported to another world," with its own meanings and an order that may or may not have much to do with the order of everyday life. As the curtain falls, the spectator "returns to reality," that is, to the paramount reality of everyday life by comparison with which the reality presented on the stage now appears tenuous and ephemeral, however vivid the presentation may have been a few moments previously. Aesthetic and religious experience is rich in producing transitions of this kind, inasmuch as art and religion are endemic producers of finite provinces of meaning.

All finite provinces of meaning are characterized by a turning away of attention from the reality of everyday life. While there are, of course, shifts in attention *within* everyday life, the shift to a finite province of meaning is of a much more radical kind. A radical change takes place in the tension of consciousness. In the context of religious experience this has been aptly called "leaping." It is important to stress, however, that the reality of everyday life retains its paramount status even as such "leaps" take place. If nothing else, language makes sure of this. The common language available to me for the objectification of my experiences is grounded in everyday life and keeps pointing back to it even as I employ it to interpret experiences in finite provinces of meaning. Typically, therefore, I "distort" the reality of the latter as soon as I begin to use the common language in interpreting them, that is, I "translate" the non-everyday experiences back into the paramount reality of everyday life. This may be readily seen in terms of dreams, but is also typical of those trying to report about theoretical, aesthetic or religious worlds of meaning. The theoretical physicist tells us that his concept of space cannot be conveyed linguistically, just as the artist does with regard to the meaning of his creations and the mystic with regard to his encounters with the divine. Yet all these—dreamer, physicist, artist and mystic—*also* live in the reality of everyday life. Indeed, one of their important problems is to interpret the coexistence of this reality with the reality enclaves into which they have ventured.

The world of everyday life is structured both spatially and temporally. The spatial structure is quite peripheral to our present considerations. Suffice it to point out that it, too, has a social dimension by virtue of the fact that my manipulatory zone intersects with that of others. More important for our present purpose is the temporal structure of everyday life.

Temporality is an intrinsic property of consciousness. The stream of consciousness is always ordered temporally. It is possible to differentiate between different levels of this temporality as it is intrasubjectively available. Every individual is conscious of an inner flow of time, which in turn is founded on the physiological rhythms of the organism though it is not identical with these. It would greatly exceed the scope of these prolegomena to enter into a detailed analysis of these levels of intrasubjective temporality. As we have indicated, however, intersubjectivity in everyday life also has a temporal dimension. The world of everyday life has its own standard time, which is intersubjectively available. This standard time may be understood as the intersection between cosmic time and its socially established calendar, based on the temporal sequences of nature, and inner time, in its aforementioned differentiations. There can never be full simultaneity between these various levels of temporality, as the experience of waiting indicates most clearly. Both my organism and my society impose upon me, and upon my inner time, certain sequences of events that involve waiting. I may want to take part in a sports event, but I must wait for my bruised knee to heal. Or again, I must wait until certain papers are processed so that my qualification for the event may be officially established. It may readily be seen that the temporal structure of everyday life is exceedingly complex, because the different levels of empirically present temporality must be ongoingly correlated.

The temporal structure of everyday life confronts me as a facticity with which I must reckon, that is, with which I must try to synchronize my own projects. I encounter time in everyday reality as continuous and finite. All my existence in this world is continuously ordered by its time, is indeed enveloped by it. My own life is an episode in the externally factitious stream of time. It was there before I was born and it will be there after I die. The knowledge of my inevitable death makes this time finite *for me*. I have only a certain amount of time available for the realization of my projects, and the knowledge of this affects my attitude to these projects. Also, since I do not want to die, this knowledge injects an underlying anxiety into my projects. Thus I cannot endlessly repeat my participation in sports events. I know that I am getting older. It may even be that this is the last occasion on which I have the chance to participate. My waiting will be anxious to the degree in which the finitude of time impinges upon the project.

The same temporal structure, as has already been indicated, is coercive. I cannot reverse at will the sequences imposed by it—"first things first" is an essential element of my knowledge of everyday life. Thus I cannot take a certain examination before I have passed through certain educational programs, I cannot practice my profession before I have taken this examination, and so on. Also, the same temporal structure provides the historicity that determines my situation in the world of everyday life. I was born on a certain date, entered school on another, started working as a professional on another, and so on. These dates, however, are all "located" within a much more comprehensive history, and this "location" decisively shapes my situation. Thus I was born in the year of the great bank crash in which my father lost his wealth, I entered school just before the revolution, I began to work just after the great war broke out, and so forth. The temporal structure of everyday life not only imposes prearranged sequences upon the "agenda" of any single day but also imposes itself upon my biography as a whole. Within the co-ordinates set by this temporal structure I apprehend both daily "agenda" and overall biography. Clock and calendar ensure that, indeed, I am a "man of my time." Only within this temporal structure does everyday life retain for me its accent of reality. Thus in cases where I may be "disoriented" for one reason or another (say, I have been in an automobile accident in which I was knocked unconscious), I feel an almost instinctive urge to "reorient" myself within the temporal structure of everyday life. I look at my watch and try to recall what day it is. By these acts alone I re-enter the reality of everyday life.

2. Social Interaction in Everyday Life

The reality of everyday life is shared with others. But how are these others themselves experienced in everyday life? Again, it is possible to differentiate between several modes of such experience.

The most important experience of others takes place in the face-to-face situation, which is the prototypical case of social interaction. All other cases are derivatives of it.

In the face-to-face situation the other is appresented to me in a vivid present shared by both of us. I know that in the same vivid present I am appresented to him. My and his "here and now" continuously impinge on each other as long as the face-to-face situation continues. As a result, there is a continuous interchange of my expressivity and his. I see him smile, then react to my frown by stopping the smile, then smiling again as I smile, and so on. Every expression of mine is oriented toward him, and vice versa, and this continuous reciprocity of expressive acts is simultaneously available to both of us. This means that, in the face-to-face situation, the other's subjectivity is available to me through a maximum of symptoms. To be sure, I may misinterpret some of these symptoms. I may think that the other is smiling while in fact he is smirking. Nevertheless, no other form of social relating can reproduce the plenitude of symptoms of subjectivity present in the face-to-face situation. Only here is the other's subjectivity emphatically "close." All other forms of relating to the other are, in varying degrees, "remote."

In the face-to-face situation the other is fully real. This reality is part of the overall reality of everyday life, and as such massive and compelling. To be sure, another may be real to me without my having encountered him face to face—by reputation, say, or by having corresponded with him. Nevertheless, he becomes real to me in the fullest sense of the word only when I meet him face to face. Indeed, it may be argued that the other in the face-to-face situation is more real to me than I myself. Of course I "know myself better" than I can ever know him. My subjectivity is accessible to me in a way his can never be, no matter how "close" our relationship. My past is available to me in memory in a fullness with which I can never reconstruct his, however much he may tell me about it. But this "better knowledge" of myself requires reflection. It is not immediately appresented to me. The other, however, *is* so appresented in the face-to-face situation. "What he is," therefore, is ongoingly available to me. This availability is continuous and prereflective. On the other hand, "What I am" is *not* so available. To make it available requires that I stop, arrest the continuous spontaneity of my experience, and deliberately turn my attention back upon myself. What is more, such reflection about myself is typically occasioned by the attitude toward me that *the other* exhibits. It is typically a "mirror" response to attitudes of the other.

It follows that relations with others in the face-to-face situation are highly flexible. Put negatively, it is comparatively difficult to impose rigid patterns upon face-to-face interaction. Whatever patterns are introduced will be continuously modified through the exceedingly variegated and subtle interchange of subjective meanings that goes on. For instance, I may view the other as someone inherently unfriendly to me and act toward him within a pattern of "unfriendly relations" as understood by me. In the face-to-face situation, however, the other may confront me with attitudes and acts that contradict this pattern, perhaps up to a point where I am led to abandon the pattern as inapplicable and to view him as friendly. In other words, the pattern cannot sustain the massive evidence of the other's subjectivity that is available to me in the face-to-face situation. By contrast, it is much easier for me to ignore such evidence as long as I do not encounter the other face to face. Even in such a relatively "close" relation as may be maintained by correspondence I can more successfully dismiss the other's protestations of friendship as not actually representing his subjective attitude to me, simply because in correspondence I lack the immediate, continuous and massively real presence of his expressivity. It is, to be sure, possible for me to misinterpret the other's meanings even in the face-to-face situation, as it is possible for him "hypocritically" to hide his meanings. All the same, both misinterpretation and "hypocrisy" are more difficult to sustain in face-to-face interaction than in less "close" forms of social relations.

On the other hand, I apprehend the other by means of typificatory schemes even in the face-to-face situation, although these schemes are more "vulnerable" to his interference than in "remoter" forms of interaction. Put differently, while it is comparatively difficult to impose rigid patterns on face-to-face interaction, even it is patterned from the beginning if it takes place within the routines of everyday life. (We can leave aside for later consideration cases of interaction between complete strangers who have no common background of everyday life.) The reality of everyday life contains typificatory schemes in terms of which others are apprehended and "dealt with" in face-to-face encounters. Thus I apprehend the other as "a man," "a European," "a buyer," "a jovial type," and so on. All these typifications ongoingly affect my interaction with him as, say, I decide to show him a good time on the town before trying to sell him my product. Our face-to-face interaction will be patterned by these typifications as long as they do not become problematic through interference on his part. Thus he may come up with evidence that, although "a man," "a European" and "a buyer," he is also a self-righteous moralist, and that what appeared first as joviality is actually an expression of contempt for Americans in general and American salesmen in particular. At this point, of course, my typificatory scheme will have to be modified, and the evening planned differently in accordance with this modification. Unless thus challenged, though, the typifications will hold until further notice and will determine my actions in the situation.

The typificatory schemes entering into face-to-face situations are, of course, reciprocal. The other also apprehends me in a typified way—as "a man," "an American," "a salesman," "an ingratiating fellow," and so on. The other's typifications are as susceptible to my interference as mine are to his. In other words, the two typificatory schemes enter into an ongoing "negotiation" in the face-to-face situation. In everyday life such "negotiation" is itself likely to be prearranged in a typical manner—as in the typical bargaining process between buyers and salesmen. Thus, most of the time, my encounters with others in everyday life are typical in a double sense—I apprehend the other as a type and I interact with him in a situation that is itself typical.

The typifications of social interaction become progressively anonymous the farther away they are from the face-to-face situation. Every typification, of course, entails incipient anonymity. If I typify my friend Henry as a member of category X (say, as an Englishman), I *ipso facto* interpret at least certain aspects of his conduct as resulting from this typification—for instance, his tastes in food are typical of Englishmen, as are his manners, certain of his emotional reactions, and so on. This implies, though, that these characteristics and actions of my friend Henry appertain to *anyone* in the category of Englishman, that is, I apprehend these aspects of his being in anonymous terms. Nevertheless, as long as my friend Henry is available in the plenitude of expressivity of the face-to-face situation, he will constantly break through my type of anonymous Englishman and manifest himself as a unique and therefore atypical individual-to wit, as my friend Henry. The anonymity of the type is obviously less susceptible to this kind of individualization when face-to-face interaction is a matter of the past (my friend Henry, *the Englishman*, whom I knew when I was a college student), or is of a superficial and transient kind (the Englishman with whom I have a brief conversation on a train), or has never taken place (my business competitors in England).

An important aspect of the experience of others in everyday life is thus the directness or indirectness of such experience. At any given time it is possible to distinguish between consociates with whom I interact in face-to-face situations and others who are mere contemporaries, of whom I have only more or less detailed recollections, or of whom I know merely by hearsay. In face-to-face situations I have direct evidence of my fellowman, of his actions, his attributes, and so on. Not so in the case of contemporaries—of them I have more or less reliable knowledge. Furthermore, I must take account of my fellowman in face-to-face situations, while I may, but need not, turn my thoughts to mere contemporaries. Anonymity increases as I go from the former to the latter, because the anonymity of the typifications by means of which I apprehend fellowmen in face-to-face situations is constantly "filled in" by the multiplicity of vivid symptoms referring to a concrete human being.

This, of course, is not the whole story. There are obvious differences in my experiences of mere contemporaries. Some I have experienced again and again in face-to-face situations and expect to meet again regularly (my friend Henry); others I *recollect* as concrete human beings from a past meeting (the blonde I passed on the street), but the meeting was brief and, most likely, will not be repeated. Still others I *know of* as concrete human beings, but I can apprehend them only by means of more or less anonymous intersecting typifications (my British business competitors, the Queen of England). Among the latter one could again distinguish between likely partners in face-to-face situations (my British business competitors), and potential but unlikely partners (the Queen of England).

The degree of anonymity characterizing the experience of others in everyday life depends, however, upon another factor too. I see the newspaper vendor on the street corner as regularly as I see my wife. But he is less important to me and I am not on intimate terms with him. He may remain relatively anonymous to me. The degree of interest and the degree of intimacy may combine to increase or decrease anonymity of experience. They may also influence it independently. I can be on fairly intimate terms with a number of the fellow-members of a tennis club and on very formal terms with my boss. Yet the former, while by no means completely anonymous, may merge into "that bunch at the courts" while the latter stands out as a unique individual. And finally, anonymity may become near-total with certain typifications that are not intended ever to become individualized—such as the "typical reader of the London *Times*." Finally, the "scope" of the typification—and thereby its anonymity—can be further increased by speaking of "British public opinion."

The social reality of everyday life is thus apprehended in a continuum of typifications, which are progressively anonymous as they are removed from the "here and now" of the face-to-face situation. At one pole of the continuum are those others with whom I frequently and intensively interact in face-to-face situations—my "inner circle," as it were. At the other pole are highly anonymous abstractions, which by their very nature can never be available in face-to-face interaction. Social structure is the sum total of these typifications and of the recurrent patterns of interaction established by means of them. As such, social structure is an essential element of the reality of everyday life.

One further point ought to be made here, though we cannot elaborate it. My relations with others are not limited to consociates and contemporaries. I also relate to predecessors and successors, to those others who have preceded and will follow me in the encompassing history of my society.

Like many classical sociologists, Karl Marx (1818–1883) was interdisciplinary, combining elements of economics, history, and philosophy to produce a body of sociological work that has not only inspired academics, but also activists and even state building. The following selection from Marx's work is drawn from the *Manifesto of the Communist Party*. Co-authored by Friedrich Engels (1820-1895), this excerpt provides a summary of Marx's theory on the development of capitalism and the fundamental inequalities upon which it rests.

Manifesto of the Communist Party

Karl Marx and Friedrich Engels

A spectre is haunting Europe—the spectre of Communism. All the Powers of old Europe have entered into a holy alliance to exorcise this spectre: Pope and Czar, Metternich and Guizot, French Radicals and German police-spies.

Where is the party in opposition that has not been decried as Communistic by its opponents in power? Where the Opposition that has not hurled back the branding reproach of Communism, against the more advanced opposition parties, as well as against its reactionary adversaries?

Two things result from this fact.

I. Communism is already acknowledged by all European Powers to be itself a Power.

II. It is high time that Communists should openly, in the face of the whole world, publish their views, their aims, their tendencies, and meet this nursery tale of the Spectre of Communism with a Manifesto of the party itself.

To this end, Communists of various nationalities have assembled in London, and sketched the following Manifesto, to be published in the English, French, German, Italian, Flemish and Danish languages.

I. Bourgeois and Proletarians[1]

The history of all hitherto existing society[2] is the history of class struggles.

Freeman and slave, patrician and plebeian, lord and serf, guild-master[3] and

[1] By bourgeoisie is meant the class of modern Capitalists, owners of the means of social production and employers of wage-labour. By proletariat, the class of modern wage-labourers who, having no means of production of their own, are reduced to selling their labour-power in order to live. [*Engels, English edition of 1888*]

[2] That is, all *written* history. In 1847, the pre-history of society, the social organisation existing previous to recorded history, was all but unknown. Since then, Haxthausen discovered common ownership of land in Russia, Maurer proved it to be the social foundation from which all Teutonic races started in history, and by and by village communities were found to be, or to have been the primitive form of society everywhere from India to Ireland. The inner organisation of this primitive Communistic society was laid bare, in its typical form, by Morgan's crowning discovery of the true nature of the *gens* and its relation to the *tribe*. With the dissolution of these primaeval communities society begins to be differentiated into separate and finally antagonistic classes. I have attempted to retrace this process of dissolution in: "Der Ursprung der Familie, des Privateigenthums und des Staats" [*The Origin of the Family, Private Property and the State*], 2nd edition, Stuttgart 1886. [*Engels, English edition of 1888*]

[3] Guild-master, that is, a full member of a guild, a master within, not a head of a guild. [*Engels, English edition of 1888*]

journeyman, in a word, oppressor and oppressed, stood in constant opposition to one another, carried on an uninterrupted, now hidden, now open fight, a fight that each time ended, either in a revolutionary re-constitution of society at large, or in the common ruin of the contending classes.

In the earlier epochs of history, we find almost everywhere a complicated arrangement of society into various orders, a manifold gradation of social rank. In ancient Rome we have patricians, knights, plebeians, slaves; in the Middle Ages, feudal lords, vassals, guild-masters, journeymen, apprentices, serfs; in almost all of these classes, again, subordinate gradations.

The modern bourgeois society that has sprouted from the ruins of feudal society has not done away with clash antagonisms. It has but established new classes, new conditions of oppression, new forms of struggle in place of the old ones.

Our epoch, the epoch of the bourgeoisie, possesses, however, this distinctive feature: it has simplified the class antagonisms: Society as a whole is more and more splitting up into two great hostile camps, into two great classes directly facing each other: Bourgeoisie and Proletariat.

From the serfs of the Middle Ages sprang the chartered burghers of the earliest towns. From these burgesses the first elements of the bourgeoisie were developed.

The discovery of America, the rounding of the Cape, opened up fresh ground for the rising bourgeoisie. The East-Indian and Chinese markets, the colonisation of America, trade with the colonies, the increase in the means of exchange and in commodities generally, gave to commerce, to navigation, to industry, an impulse never before known, and thereby, to the revolutionary element in the tottering feudal society, a rapid development.

The feudal system of industry, under which industrial production was monopolised by closed guilds, now no longer sufficed for the growing wants of the new markets. The manufacturing system took its place. The guild-masters were pushed on one side by the manufacturing middle class; division of labour between the different corporate guilds vanished in the face of division of labour in each single workshop.

Meantime the markets kept ever growing, the demand ever rising. Even manufacture no longer sufficed. Thereupon, steam and machinery revolutionised industrial production. The place of manufacture was taken by the giant, Modern Industry, the place of the industrial middle class, by industrial millionaires, the leaders of whole industrial armies, the modern bourgeois.

Modern industry has established the world-market, for which the discovery of America paved the way. This market has given an immense development to commerce, to navigation, to communication by land. This development has, in its turn, reacted on the extension of industry; and in proportion as industry, commerce, navigation, railways extended, in the same proportion the bourgeoisie developed, increased its capital, and pushed into the background every class handed down from the Middle Ages.

We see, therefore, how the modern bourgeoisie is itself the product of a long course of development, of a series of revolutions in the modes of production and of exchange.

Each step in the development of the bourgeoisie was accompanied by a corresponding political advance of that class. An oppressed class under the sway of the feudal nobility, an armed and self-governing association in the mediaeval commune;[4] here independent urban republic (as in Italy and Germany), there taxable "third estate" of the monarchy (as in France), afterwards, in the period of manufacture proper, serving either the semi-feudal or the absolute monarchy as a counterpoise against the nobility, and, in fact, corner-stone of the great monarchies in general, the bourgeoisie has at last, since the establishment of Modern Industry and of the world-market, conquered for itself, in the modern representative State, exclusive political sway. The executive of the modern State is but a committee for managing the common affairs of the whole bourgeoisie.

The bourgeoisie, historically, has played a most revolutionary part.

The bourgeoisie, wherever it has got the upper hand, has put an end to all feudal, patriarchal, idyllic relations. It has pitilessly torn asunder the motley feudal ties that bound man to his "natural superiors," and has left remaining no other nexus between man and man than naked self-interest, than callous "cash payment." It has drowned the most heavenly ecstasies of religious fervour, of chivalrous enthusiasm, of philistine sentimentalism, in the icy water of egotistical calculation. It has resolved personal worth into exchange value, and in place of the numberless indefeasible chartered freedoms, has set up that single, unconscionable freedom—Free Trade. In one word, for exploitation, veiled by religious and political illusions, it has substituted naked, shameless, direct, brutal exploitation.

The bourgeoisie has stripped of its halo every occupation hitherto honoured and looked up to with reverent awe. It has converted the physician, the lawyer, the priest, the poet, the man of science, into its paid wage-labourers.

The bourgeoisie has torn away from the family its sentimental veil, and has reduced the family relation to a mere money relation.

The bourgeoisie has disclosed how it came to pass that the brutal display of vigour in the Middle Ages, which Reactionists so much admire, found its fitting complement in the most slothful indolence. It has been the first to show what man's activity can bring about. It has accomplished wonders far surpassing Egyptian pyramids, Roman aqueducts, and Gothic cathedrals; it has conducted expeditions that put in the shade all former Exoduses of nations and crusades.

The bourgeoisie cannot exist without constantly revolutionising the instruments of production, and thereby the relations of production, and with them the whole relations of society. Conservation of the old modes of production in unaltered form, was, on the contrary, the first condition of existence for all earlier industrial classes. Constant revolutionising of production, uninterrupted distur-

[4] "Commune" was the name taken, in France, by the nascent towns even before they had conquered from their feudal lords and masters local self-government and political rights as the "Third Estate." Generally speaking, for the economical development of the bourgeoisie, England is here taken as the typical country; for its political development, France. [*Engels, English edition of 1888*]

This was the name given their urban communities by the townsmen of Italy and France, after they had purchased or wrested their initial rights of self-government from their feudal lords. [*Engels, German edition of 1890*]

bance of all social conditions, everlasting uncertainty and agitation distinguish the bourgeois epoch from all earlier ones. All fixed, fast-frozen relations, with their train of ancient and venerable prejudices and opinions, are swept away, all new-formed ones become antiquated before they can ossify. All that is solid melts into air, all that is holy is profaned, and man is at last compelled to face with sober senses, his real conditions of life, and his relations with his kind.

The need of a constantly expanding market for its products chases the bourgeoisie over the whole surface of the globe. It must nestle everywhere, settle everywhere, establish connexions everywhere.

The bourgeoisie has through its exploitation of the world-market given a cosmopolitan character to production and consumption in every country. To the great chagrin of Reactionists, it has drawn from under the feet of industry the national ground on which it stood. All old-established national industries have been destroyed or are daily being destroyed. They are dislodged by new industries, whose introduction becomes a life and death question for all civilised nations, by industries that no longer work up indigenous raw material, but raw material drawn from the remotest zones; industries whose products are consumed, not only at home, but in every quarter of the globe. In place of the old wants, satisfied by the productions of the country, we find new wants, requiring for their satisfaction the products of distant lands and climes. In place of the old local and national seclusion and self-sufficiency, we have intercourse in every direction, universal inter-dependence of nations. And as in material, so also in intellectual production. The intellectual creations of individual nations become common property. National one-sidedness and narrow-mindedness become more and more impossible, and from the numerous national and local literatures, there arises a world literature.

The bourgeoisie, by the rapid improvement of all instruments of production, by the immensely facilitated means of communication, draws all, even the most barbarian, nations into civilisation. The cheap prices of its commodities are the heavy artillery with which it batters down all Chinese walls, with which it forces the barbarians' intensely obstinate hatred of foreigners to capitulate. It compels all nations, on pain of extinction, to adopt the bourgeois mode of production; it compels them to introduce what it calls civilisation into their midst, i.e., to become bourgeois themselves. In one word, it creates a world after its own image.

The bourgeoisie has subjected the country to the rule of the towns. It has created enormous cities, has greatly increased the urban population as compared with the rural, and has thus rescued a considerable part of the population from the idiocy of rural life. Just as it has made the country dependent on the towns, so it has made barbarian and semi-barbarian countries dependent on the civilised ones, nations of peasants on nations of bourgeois, the East on the West.

The bourgeoisie keeps more and more doing away with the scattered state of the population, of the means of production, and of property. It has agglomerated population, centralised means of production, and has concentrated property in a few hands. The necessary consequence of this was political centralisation. Independent, or but loosely connected provinces, with separate interests, laws, governments and systems of taxation, became lumped together into one nation, with one government, one code of laws, one national class-interest, one frontier and one customs-tariff.

The bourgeoisie, during its rule of scarce one hundred years, has created more massive and more colossal productive forces than have all preceding generations together. Subjection of Nature's forces to man, machinery, application of chemistry to industry and agriculture, steam-navigation, railways, electric telegraphs, clearing of whole continents for cultivation, canalisation of rivers, whole populations conjured out of the ground—what earlier century had even a presentiment that such productive forces slumbered in the lap of social labour?

We see then: the means of production and of exchange, on whose foundation the bourgeoisie built itself up, were generated in feudal society. At a certain stage in the development of these means of production and of exchange, the conditions under which feudal society produced and exchanged, the feudal organisation of agriculture and manufacturing industry, in one word, the feudal relations of property became no longer compatible with the already developed productive forces; they became so many fetters. They had to be burst asunder; they were burst asunder.

Into their place stepped free competition, accompanied by a social and political constitution adapted to it, and by the economical and political sway of the bourgeois class.

A similar movement is going on before our own eyes. Modern bourgeois society with its relations of production, of exchange and of property, a society that has conjured up such gigantic means of production and of exchange, is like the sorcerer, who is no longer able to control the powers of the nether world whom he has called up by his spells. For many a decade past the history of industry and commerce is but the history of the revolt of modern productive forces against modern conditions of production, against the property relations that are the conditions for the existence of the bourgeoisie and of its rule. It is enough to mention the commercial crises that by their periodical return put on its trial, each time more threateningly, the existence of the entire bourgeois society. In these crises a great part not only of the existing products, but also of the previously created productive forces, are periodically destroyed. In these crises there breaks out an epidemic that, in all earlier epochs, would have seemed an absurdity—the epidemic of over-production. Society suddenly finds itself put back into a state of momentary barbarism; it appears as if a famine, a universal war of devastation had cut off the supply of every means of subsistence; industry and commerce seem to be destroyed; and why? Because there is too much civilisation, too much means of subsistence, too much industry, too much commerce. The productive forces at the disposal of society no longer tend to further the development of the conditions of bourgeois property; on the contrary, they have become too powerful for these conditions, by which they are fettered, and so soon as they overcome these fetters, they bring disorder into the whole of bourgeois society, endanger the existence of bourgeois property. The conditions of bourgeois society are too narrow to comprise the wealth created by them. And how does the bourgeoisie get over these crises? On the one hand by enforced destruction of a mass of productive forces; on the other, by the conquest of new markets, and by the more thorough exploitation of the old ones. That is to say, by paving the way for more extensive and more destructive crises, and by diminishing the means whereby crises are prevented.

The weapons with which the bourgeoisie felled feudalism to the ground are now turned against the bourgeoisie itself.

But not only has the bourgeoisie forged the weapons that bring death to itself; it has also called into existence the men who are to wield those weapons—the modern working class—the proletarians.

In proportion as the bourgeoisie, i.e., capital, is developed, in the same proportion is the proletariat, the modern working class, developed—a class of labourers, who live only so long as they find work, and who find work only so long as their labour increases capital. These labourers, who must sell themselves piece-meal, are a commodity, like every other article of commerce, and are consequently exposed to all the vicissitudes of competition, to all the fluctuations of the market.

Owing to the extensive use of machinery and to division of labour, the work of the proletarians has lost all individual character, and consequently, all charm for the workman. He becomes an appendage of the machine, and it is only the most simple, most monotonous, and most easily acquired knack, that is required of him. Hence, the cost of production of a workman is restricted, almost entirely, to the means of subsistence that he requires for his maintenance, and for the propagation of his race. But the price of a commodity, and therefore also of labour is equal to its cost of production. In proportion, therefore, as the repulsiveness of the work increases, the wage decreases. Nay more, in proportion as the use of machinery and division of labour increases, in the same proportion the burden of toil also increases, whether by prolongation of the working hours, by increase of the work exacted in a given time or by increased speed of the machinery, etc.

Modern industry has converted the little workshop of the patriarchal master into the great factory of the industrial capitalist. Masses of labourers, crowded into the factory, are organised like soldiers. As privates of the industrial army they are placed under the command of a perfect hierarchy of officers and sergeants. Not only are they slaves of the bourgeois class, and of the bourgeois State; they are daily and hourly enslaved by the machine, by the over-looker, and, above all, by the individual bourgeois manufacturer himself. The more openly this despotism proclaims gain to be its end and aim, the more petty, the more hateful and the more embittering it is.

The less the skill and exertion of strength implied in manual labour, in other words, the more modern industry becomes developed, the more is the labour of men superseded by that of women. Differences of age and sex have no longer any distinctive social validity for the working class. All are instruments of labour, more or less expensive to use, according to their age and sex.

No sooner is the exploitation of the labourer by the manufacturer, so far, at an end, that he receives his wages in cash, than he is set upon by the other portions of the bourgeoisie, the landlord, the shopkeeper, the pawnbroker, etc.

The lower strata of the middle class—the small tradespeople, shopkeepers, and retired tradesmen generally, the handicraftsmen and peasants—all these sink gradually into the proletariat, partly because their diminutive capital does not suffice for the scale on which Modern Industry is carried on, and is swamped in the competition with the large capitalists, partly because their specialised skill is rendered worthless by new methods of production. Thus the proletariat is recruited from all classes of the population.

The proletariat goes through various stages of development. With its birth begins its struggle with the bourgeoisie. At first the contest is carried on by individual labourers, then by the workpeople of a factory, then by the operatives of one trade, in one locality, against the individual bourgeois who directly exploits them. They direct their attacks not against the bourgeois conditions of production, but against the instruments of production themselves; they destroy imported wares that compete with their labour, they smash to pieces machinery, they set factories ablaze, they seek to restore by force the vanished status of the workman of the Middle Ages.

At this stage the labourers still form an incoherent mass scattered over the whole country, and broken up by their mutual competition. If anywhere they unite to form more compact bodies, this is not yet the consequence of their own active union, but of the union of the bourgeoisie, which class, in order to attain its own political ends, is compelled to set the whole proletariat in motion, and is moreover yet, for a time, able to do so. At this stage, therefore, the proletarians do not fight their enemies, but the enemies of their enemies, the remnants of absolute monarchy, the landowners, the non-industrial bourgeois, the petty bourgeoisie. Thus the whole historical movement is concentrated in the hands of the bourgeoisie; every victory so obtained is a victory for the bourgeoisie.

But with the development of industry the proletariat not only increases in number; it becomes concentrated in greater masses, its strength grows, and it feels that strength more. The various interests and conditions of life within the ranks of the proletariat are more and more equalised, in proportion as machinery obliterates all distinctions of labour, and nearly everywhere reduces wages to the same low level. The growing competition among the bourgeois, and the resulting commercial crises, make the wages of the workers ever more fluctuating. The unceasing improvement of machinery, ever more rapidly developing, makes their livelihood more and more precarious; the collisions between individual workmen and individual bourgeois take more and more the character of collisions between two classes. Thereupon the workers begin to form combinations (Trades Unions) against the bourgeois; they club together in order to keep up the rate of wages; they found permanent associations in order to make provision beforehand for these occasional revolts. Here and there the contest breaks out into riots.

Now and then the workers are victorious, but only for a time. The real fruit of their battles lies, not in the immediate result, but in the ever-expanding union of the workers. This union is helped on by the improved means of communication that are created by modern industry and that place the workers of different localities in contact with one another. It was just this contact that was needed to centralise the numerous local struggles, all of the same character, into one national struggle between classes. But every class struggle is a political struggle. And that union, to attain which the burghers of the Middle Ages, with their miserable highways, required centuries, the modern proletarians, thanks to railways, achieve in a few years.

This organisation of the proletarians into a class, and consequently into a political party, is continually being upset again by the competition between the workers themselves. But it ever rises up again, stronger, firmer, mightier. It compels legislative recognition of particular interests of the workers, by taking advantage of the divisions among the bourgeoisie itself. Thus the ten-hours' bill in England was carried.

Altogether collisions between the classes of the old society further, in many ways, the course of development of the proletariat. The bourgeoisie finds itself involved in a constant battle. At first with the aristocracy; later on, with those portions of the bourgeoisie itself, whose interests have become antagonistic to the progress of industry; at all times, with the bourgeoisie of foreign countries. In all these battles it sees itself compelled to appeal to the proletariat, to ask for its help, and thus, to drag it into the political arena. The bourgeoisie itself, therefore, supplies the proletariat with its own elements of political and general education, in other words, it furnishes the proletariat with weapons for fighting the bourgeoisie.

Further, as we have already seen, entire sections of the ruling classes are, by the advance of industry, precipitated into the proletariat, or are at least threatened in their conditions of existence. These also supply the proletariat with fresh elements of enlightenment and progress.

Finally, in times when the class struggle nears the decisive hour, the process of dissolution going on within the ruling class, in fact within the whole range of society, assumes such a violent, glaring character, that a small section of the ruling class cuts itself adrift, and joins the revolutionary class, the class that holds the future in its hands. Just as, therefore, at an earlier period, a section of the nobility went over to the bourgeoisie, so now a portion of the bourgeoisie goes over to the proletariat, and in particular, a portion of the bourgeois ideologists, who have raised themselves to the level of comprehending theoretically the historical movement as a whole.

Of all the classes that stand face to face with the bourgeoisie today, the proletariat alone is a really revolutionary class. The other classes decay and finally disappear in the face of Modern Industry; the proletariat is its special and essential product.

The lower middle class, the small manufacturer, the shopkeeper, the artisan, the peasant, all these fight against the bourgeoisie, to save from extinction their existence as fractions of the middle class. They are therefore not revolutionary, but conservative. Nay more, they are reactionary, for they try to roll back the wheel of history. If by chance they are revolutionary, they are so only in view of their impending transfer into the proletariat, they thus defend not their present, but their future interests, they desert their own standpoint to place themselves at that of the proletariat.

The "dangerous class," the social scum, that passively rotting mass thrown off by the lowest layers of old society, may, here and there, be swept into the movement by a proletarian revolution; its conditions of life, however, prepare it far more for the part of a bribed tool of reactionary intrigue.

In the conditions of the proletariat, those of old society at large are already virtually swamped. The proletarian is without property; his relation to his wife and children has no longer anything in common with the bourgeois family-relations; modern industrial labour, modern subjection to capital, the same in England as in France, in America as in Germany, has stripped him of every trace of national character. Law, morality, religion, are to him so many bourgeois prejudices, behind which lurk in ambush just as many bourgeois interests.

All the preceding classes that got the upper hand, sought to fortify their already acquired status by subjecting society at large to their conditions of appropriation. The proletarians cannot become masters of the productive forces of society, except by abolishing their own previous mode of appropriation, and thereby also every other previous mode of appropriation. They have nothing of their own to secure and to fortify; their mission is to destroy all previous securities for, and insurances of, individual property.

All previous historical movements were movements of minorities, or in the interests of minorities. The proletarian movement is the self-conscious, independent movement of the immense majority, in the interests of the immense majority. The proletariat, the lowest stratum of our present society, cannot stir, cannot raise itself up, without the whole superincumbent strata of official society being sprung into the air.

Though not in substance, yet in form, the struggle of the proletariat with the bourgeoisie is at first a national struggle. The proletariat of each country must, of course, first of all settle matters with its own bourgeoisie.

In depicting the most general phases of the development of the proletariat, we traced the more or less veiled civil war, raging within existing society, up to the point where that war breaks out into open revolution, and where the violent overthrow of the bourgeoisie lays the foundation for the sway of the proletariat.

Hitherto, every form of society has been based, as we have already seen, on the antagonism of oppressing and oppressed classes. But in order to oppress a class, certain conditions must be assured to it under which it can, at least, continue its slavish existence. The serf, in the period of serfdom, raised himself to membership in the commune, just as the petty bourgeois, under the yoke of feudal absolutism, managed to develop into a bourgeois. The modern labourer, on the contrary, instead of rising with the progress of industry, sinks deeper and deeper below the conditions of existence of his own class. He becomes a pauper, and pauperism develops more rapidly than population and wealth. And here it becomes evident, that the bourgeoisie is unfit any longer to be the ruling class in society, and to impose its conditions of existence upon society as an over-riding law. It is unfit to rule because it is incompetent to assure an existence to its slave within his slavery, because it cannot help letting him sink into such a state, that it has to feed him, instead of being fed by him. Society can no longer live under this bourgeoisie, in other words, its existence is no longer compatible with society.

The essential condition for the existence, and for the sway of the bourgeois class, is the formation and augmentation of capital; the condition for capital is wage-labour. Wage-labour rests exclusively on competition between the labourers. The advance of industry, whose involuntary promoter is the bourgeoisie, replaces the isolation of the labourers, due to competition, by their revolutionary combination, due to association. The development of Modern Industry, therefore, cuts from under its feet the very foundation on which the bourgeoisie produces and appropriates products. What the bourgeoisie, therefore, produces, above all, is its own grave-diggers. Its fall and the victory of the proletariat are equally inevitable.

Max Weber (1864–1920) is clearly among the giants in sociology. His voluminous scholarship on politics, economy, history, methodology, rationality, and bureaucracy has directly influenced many areas of sociology. Weber was especially interested in cross-cultural research, and sought to identify the causes of variations in political and economic development over time and space. The following selection is from his book *The Protestant Ethic and the Spirit of Capitalism*, wherein Weber examines the "spirit" behind the development of Western style capitalism as it relates to religious values and beliefs, particularly those of Calvinism.

The Protestant Ethic and the Spirit of Capitalism

Max Weber

In the title of this study is used the somewhat pretentious phrase, the *spirit* of capitalism. What is to be understood by it? The attempt to give anything like a definition of it brings out certain difficulties which are in the very nature of this type of investigation.

If any object can be found to which this term can be applied with any understandable meaning, it can only be an historical individual, i.e. a complex of elements associated in historical reality which we unite into a conceptual whole from the standpoint of their cultural significance.

Such an historical concept, however, since it refers in its content to a phenomenon significant for its unique individuality, cannot be defined according to the formula *genus proximum, differentia specifica,* but it must be gradually put together out of the individual parts which are taken from historical reality to make it up. Thus the final and definitive concept cannot stand at the beginning of the investigation, but must come at the end. We must, in other words, work out in the course of the discussion, as its most important result, the best conceptual formulation of what we here understand by the spirit of capitalism, that is the best from the point of view which interests us here. This point of view (the one of which we shall speak later) is, further, by no means the only possible one from which the historical phenomena we are investigating can be analysed. Other standpoints would, for this as for every historical phenomenon, yield other characteristics as the essential ones. The result is that it is by no means necessary to understand by the spirit of capitalism only what it will come to mean to *us* for the purposes of our analysis. This is a necessary result of the nature of historical concepts which attempt for their methodological purposes not to grasp historical reality in abstract general formulæ, but in concrete genetic sets of relations which are inevitably of a specifically unique and individual character.[1]

Thus, if we try to determine the object, the analysis and historical explanation of which we are attempting, it cannot be in the form of a conceptual definition, but at least in the beginning only a provisional description of what is here meant by the spirit of capitalism. Such a description is, however, indispensable in order clearly to understand the object of the investigation. For this purpose we turn to a document of that spirit which contains what we are looking for in almost classical purity, and at the same time has the advantage of being free from all direct relationship to religion, being thus, for our purposes, free of preconceptions.

> "Remember, that *time* is money. He that can earn ten shillings a day by his labour, and goes abroad, or sits idle, one half of that day, though he spends but sixpence during his diversion or idleness, ought not to reckon *that* the only expense; he has really spent, or rather thrown away, five shillings besides.
>
> "Remember, that *credit* is money. If a man lets his money lie in my hands after it is due, he gives me the interest, or so much as I can make of it during that time. This amounts to a considerable sum where a man has good and large credit, and makes good use of it.
>
> "Remember, that money is of the prolific, generating nature. Money can beget money, and its offspring can beget more, and so on. Five shillings turned is six, turned again it is seven and threepence, and so on, till it becomes a hundred pounds. The more there is of it, the more it produces every turning, so that the profits rise quicker and quicker. He that kills a breeding-sow, destroys all her offspring to the thousandth generation. He that murders a crown, destroys all that it might have produced, even scores of pounds."
>
> "Remember this saying, *The good paymaster is lord of another man's purse*. He that is known to pay punctually and exactly to the time he promises, may at any time, and on any occasion, raise all the money his friends can spare. This is sometimes of great use. After industry and frugality, nothing contributes more to the raising of a young man in the world than punctuality and justice in all his dealings; therefore never keep borrowed money an hour beyond the time you promised, lest a disappointment shut up your friend's purse for ever.
>
> "The most trifling actions that affect a man's credit are to be regarded. The sound of your hammer at five in the morning, or eight at night, heard by a creditor, makes him easy six months longer; but if he sees you at a billiard-

---

[1] These passages represent a very brief summary of some aspects of Weber's methodological views. At about the same time that he wrote this essay he was engaged in a thorough criticism and revaluation of the methods of the Social Sciences, the result of which was a point of view in many ways different from the prevaling one, especially outside of Germany. In order thoroughly to understand the significance of this essay in its wider bearings on Weber's sociological work as a whole it is necessary to know what his methodological aims were. Most of his writings on this subject have been assembled since his death (in 1920) in the volume *Gesammelte Aufsätze zur Wissenschaftslehre*. A shorter exposition of the main position is contained in the opening chapters of *Wirtschaft und Gesellschaft, Grundriss der Sozialökonomik, III*. —Translator's Note.

table, or hears your voice at a tavern, when you should be at work, he sends for his money the next day; demands it, before he can receive it, in a lump.

"It shows, besides, that you are mindful of what you owe; it makes you appear a careful as well as an honest man, and that still increases your credit.

"Beware of thinking all your own that you possess, and of living accordingly. It is a mistake that many people who have credit fall into. To prevent this, keep an exact account for some time both of your expenses and your income. If you take the pains at first to mention particulars, it will have this good effect: you will discover how wonderfully small, trifling expenses mount up to large sums, and will discern what might have been, and may for the future be saved, without occasioning any great inconvenience."

"For six pounds a year you may have the use of one hundred pounds, provided you are a man of known prudence and honesty.

"He that spends a groat a day idly, spends idly above six pounds a year, which is the price for the use of one hundred pounds.

"He that wastes idly a groat's worth of his time per day, one day with another, wastes the privilege of using one hundred pounds each day.

"He that idly loses five shillings' worth of time, loses five shillings, and might as prudently throw five shillings into the sea.

"He that loses five shillings, not only loses that sum, but all the advantage that might be made by turning it in dealing, which by the time that a young man becomes old, will amount to a considerable sum of money."[2]

It is Benjamin Franklin who preaches to us in these sentences, the same which Ferdinand Kürnberger satirizes in his clever and malicious *Picture of American Culture*[3] as the supposed confession of faith of the Yankee. That it is the spirit of capitalism which here speaks in characteristic fashion, no one will doubt, however little we may wish to claim that everything which could be understood as pertaining to that spirit is contained in it. Let us pause a moment to consider this passage, the philosophy of which Kürnberger sums up in the words, "They make tallow out of cattle and money out of men". The peculiarity of this philosophy of avarice appears to be the ideal of the honest man of recognized credit, and above all the idea of a duty of the individual toward the increase of his capital, which is assumed as an end in itself. Truly what is here preached is not simply a means of making one's way in the world, but a peculiar ethic. The infraction of its rules is treated not as foolishness but as forgetfulness of duty. That is the essence of the matter. It is not mere business astuteness, that sort of thing is common enough, it is an ethos. *This* is the quality which interests us.

[2] The final passage is from *Necessary Hints to Those That Would Be Rich* (written in 1736, Works, Sparks edition, II, p. 80), the rest from *Advice to a Young Tradesman* (written 1748, Sparks edition, II, pp. 87 ff.). The italics in the text are Franklin's.

[3] *Der Amerikamüde* (Frankfurt, 1855), well known to be an imaginative paraphrase of Lenau's impressions of America. As a work of art the book would to-day be somewhat difficult to enjoy, but it is incomparable as a document of the (now long since blurred-over) differences between the German and the American outlook, one may even say of the type of spiritual life which, in spite of everything, has remained common to all Germans, Catholic and Protestant alike, since the German mysticism of the Middle Ages, as against the Puritan capitalistic valuation of action.

When Jacob Fugger, in speaking to a business associate who had retired and who wanted to persuade him to do the same, since he had made enough money and should let others have a chance, rejected that as pusillanimity and answered that "he (Fugger) thought otherwise, he wanted to make money as long as he could",[4] the spirit of his statement is evidently quite different from that of Franklin. What in the former case was an expression of commercial daring and a personal inclination morally neutral,[5] in the latter takes on the character of an ethically coloured maxim for the conduct of life. The concept spirit of capitalism is here used in this specific sense,[6] it is the spirit of modern capitalism. For that we are here dealing only with Western European and American capitalism is obvious from the way in which the problem was stated. Capitalism existed in China, India, Babylon, in the classic world, and in the Middle Ages. But in all these cases, as we shall see, this particular ethos was lacking.

Now, all Franklin's moral attitudes are coloured with utilitarianism. Honesty is useful, because it assures credit; so are punctuality, industry, frugality, and that is the reason they are virtues. A logical deduction from this would be that where, for instance, the appearance of honesty serves the same purpose, that would suffice, and an unnecessary surplus of this virtue would evidently appear to Franklin's eyes as unproductive waste. And as a matter of fact, the story in his autobiography of his conversion to those virtues,[7] or the discussion of the value of a strict maintenance of the appearance of modesty, the assiduous belittlement of one's own deserts in order to gain general recognition later,[8] con-

[4] Sombart has used this quotation as a motto for his section dealing with the genesis of capitalism (*Der moderne Kaptialismus*, first edition, I, p. 193. See also p. 390).

[5] Which quite obviously does not mean either that Jacob Frugger was a morally indifferent or an irreligious man, or that Benjamin Franklin's ethic is completely covered by the above quotations. It scarcely required Brentano's quotations (*Die Anfänge des modernen Kapitalismus*, pp. 150 ff.) to protect this well-known philanthropist from the misunderstanding which Brentano seems to attribute to me. The problem is just the reverse: how could such a philanthropist come to write these particular sentences (the especially characteristic form of which Brentano has neglected to reproduce) in the manner of a moralist?

[6] This is the basis of our difference from Sombart in stating the problem. Its very considerable practical significance will become clear later. In anticipation, however, let it be remarked that Sombart has by no means neglected this ethical aspect of the capitalistic entrepreneur. But in his view of the problem it appears as a result of capitalism, whereas for our purposes we must assume the opposite as an hypothesis. A final position can only be taken up at the end of the investigation. For Sombart's view see *op. cit.*, pp. 357, 380, etc. His reasoning here connects with the brilliant analysis given in Simmel's *Philosophie des Geldes* (final chapter). Of the polemics which he has brought forward against me in his *Bourgeios* I shall come to speak later. At this point any thorough discussion must be postponed.

[7] "I grew convinced that truth, sincerity, and integrity in dealings between man and man were of the utmost importance to the felicity of life; and I formed written resolutions, which still remain in my journal book to practice them ever while I lived. Revelation had indeed no weight with me as such; but I entertained an opinion that though certain actions might not be bad because they were forbidden by it, or good because it commanded them, yet probably these actions might be forbidden because they were bad for us, or commanded because they were beneficial to us in their own nature, all the circumstances of things considered." *Autobiography* (ed. F. W. Pine, Henry Holt, New York, 1916), p. 112.

[8] "I therefore put myself as much as I could out of sight and started it"—that is the project of a library which he had initiated—"as a scheme of a *number of friends*, who had requested me to go about and propose it to such as they thought lovers of reading. In this way my affair went on smoothly, and I ever after practiced it on such occasions; and from my frequent successes, can heartily recommend it. The present little sacrifice of your vanity will afterwards be amply repaid. If it remains awhile uncertain to whom the merit belongs, someone more vain than yourself will be encouraged to claim it, and then even envy will be disposed to do you justice by plucking those assumed feathers and restoring them to their right owner." *Autobiography*, p. 140.

firms this impression. According to Franklin, those virtues, like all others, are only in so far virtues as they are actually useful to the individual, and the surrogate of mere appearance is always sufficient when it accomplishes the end in view. It is a conclusion which is inevitable for strict utilitarianism. The impression of many Germans that the virtues professed by Americanism are pure hypocrisy seems to have been confirmed by this striking case. But in fact the matter is not by any means so simple. Benjamin Franklin's own character, as it appears in the really unusual candidness of his autobiography, belies that suspicion. The circumstance that he ascribes his recognition of the utility of virtue to a divine revelation which was intended to lead him in the path of righteousness, shows that something more than mere garnishing for purely egocentric motives is involved.

In fact, the *summum bonum* of this ethic, the earning of more and more money, combined with the strict avoidance of all spontaneous enjoyment of life, is above all completely devoid of any eudaemonistic, not to say hedonistic, admixture. It is thought of so purely as an end in itself, that from the point of view of the happiness of, or utility to, the single individual, it appears entirely transcendental and absolutely irrational.[9] Man is dominated by the making of money, by acquisition as the ultimate purpose of his life. Economic acquisition is no longer subordinated to man as the means for the satisfaction of his material needs. This reversal of what we should call the natural relationship, so irrational from a naïve point of view, is evidently as definitely a leading principle of capitalism as it is foreign to all peoples not under capitalistic influence. At the same time it expresses a type of feeling which is closely connected with certain religious ideas. If we thus ask, *why* should "money be made out of men", Benjamin Franklin himself, although he was a colourless deist, answers in his autobiography with a quotation from the Bible, which his strict Calvinistic father drummed into him again and again in his youth: "Seest thou a man diligent in his business? He shall stand before kings" (Prov. xxii. 29). The earning of money within the modern economic order is, so long as it is done legally, the result and the expression of virtue and proficiency in a calling; and this virtue and proficiency are, as it is now not difficult to see, the real Alpha and Omega of Franklin's ethic, as expressed in the passages we have quoted, as well as in all his works without exception.[10]

And in truth this peculiar idea, so familiar to us to-day, but in reality so little a matter of course, of one's duty in a calling, is what is most characteristic of the social ethic of capitalistic culture, and is in a sense the fundamental basis of

---

[9] Brentano (*op. cit.*, pp. 125, 127, note 1) takes this remark as an occasion to criticize the later discussions of "that rationalization and discipline" to which worldly asceticism has subjected men. That, he says, is a rationalization toward an irrational mode of life. He is, in fact, quite correct. A thing is never irrational in itself, but only from a particular rational point of view. For the unbeliever every religious way of life is irrational, for the hedonist every ascetic standard, no matter whether measured with respect to its particular basic values, that opposing asceticism is a rationalization. If this essay makes any contribution at all, may it be to bring out the complexity of the only superficially simple concept of the rational.

[10] In reply to Brentano's (*Die Anfänge des modernen Kapitalismus*, pp. 150 ff.) long and somewhat inaccurate apologia for Franklin, whose ethical qualities I am supposed to have misunderstood, I refer only to this statement, which should, in my opinion, have been sufficient to make that apologia superfluous.

it. It is an obligation which the individual is supposed to feel and does feel towards the content of his professional[11] activity, no matter in what it consists, in particular no matter whether it appears on the surface as a utilization of his personal powers, or only of his material possessions (as capital).

Of course, this conception has not appeared only under capitalistic conditions. On the contrary, we shall later trace its origins back to a time previous to the advent of capitalism. Still less, naturally, do we maintain that a conscious acceptance of these ethical maxims on the part of the individuals, entrepreneurs or labourers, in modern capitalistic enterprises, is a condition of the further existence of present-day capitalism. The capitalistic economy of the present day is an immense cosmos into which the individual is born, and which presents itself to him, at least as an individual, as an unalterable order of things in which he must live. It forces the individual, in so far as he is involved in the system of market relationships, to conform to capitalistic rules of action. The manufacturer who in the long run acts counter to these norms, will just as inevitably be eliminated from the economic scene as the worker who cannot or will not adapt himself to them will be thrown into the streets without a job.

Thus the capitalism of to-day, which has come to dominate economic life, educates and selects the economic subjects which it needs through a process of economic survival of the fittest. But here one can easily see the limits of the concept of selection as a means of historical explanation. In order that a manner of life so well adapted to the peculiarities of capitalism could be selected at all, i.e. should come to dominate others, it had to originate somewhere, and not in isolated individuals alone, but as a way of life common to whole groups of men. This origin is what really needs explanation. Concerning the doctrine of the more naïve historical materialism, that such ideas originate as a reflection or superstructure of economic situations, we shall speak more in detail below. At this point it will suffice for our purpose to call attention to the fact that without doubt, in the country of Benjamin Franklin's birth (Massachusetts), the spirit of capitalism (in the sense we have attached to it) was present before the capitalistic order. There were complaints of a peculiarly calculating sort of profit-seeking in New England, as distinguished from other parts of America, as early as 1632. It is further undoubted that capitalism remained far less developed in some of the neighbouring colonies, the later Southern States of the United States of America, in spite of the fact that these latter were founded by large capitalists for business motives, while the New England colonies were founded by preachers and seminary graduates with the help of small bourgeois, craftsmen and yoemen, for religious reasons. In this case the causal relation is certainly the reverse of that suggested by the materialistic standpoint.

But the origin and history of such ideas is much more complex than the theorists of the superstructure suppose. The spirit of capitalism, in the sense in

[11] The two terms profession and calling I have used in translation of the German *Beruf*, whichever seemed best to fit the particular context. Vocation does not carry the ethical connotation in which Weber is interested. It is especially to be remembered that profession in the sense it is not contrasted with business, but it refers to a particular attitude toward one's occupation, no matter what that occupation may be. This should become abundantly clear from the whole of Weber's argument. -Translator's Note.

which we are using the term, had to fight its way to supremacy against a whole world of hostile forces. A state of mind such as that expressed in the passages we have quoted from Franklin, and which called forth the applause of a whole people, would both in ancient times and in the Middle Ages[12] have been proscribed as the lowest sort of avarice and as an attitude entirely lacking in self-respect. It is, in fact, still regularly thus looked upon by all those social groups which are least involved in or adapted to modern capitalistic conditions. This is not wholly because the instinct of acquisition was in those times unknown or undeveloped, as has often been said. Nor because the *auri sacra fames*, the greed for gold, was then, or now, less powerful outside of bourgeois capitalism than within its peculiar sphere, as the illusions of modern romanticists are wont to believe. The difference between the capitalistic and precapitalistic spirits is not to be found at this point. The greed of the Chinese Mandarin, the old Roman aristocrat, or the modern peasant, can stand up to any comparison. And the *auri sacra fames* of a Neapolitan cab-driver or *barcaiuolo*, and certainly of Asiatic representatives of similar trades, as well as of the craftsmen of southern European of Asiatic countries, is, as anyone can find out for himself, very much more intense, and especially more unscrupulous than that of, say, an Englishman in similar circumstances.[13] . . .

. . . One of the fundamental elements of the spirit of modern capitalism, and not only of that but of all modern culture: rational conduct on the basis of the idea of the calling, was born—that is what this discussion has sought to demonstrate—from the spirit of Christian asceticism. One has only to re-read the passage from Franklin, quoted at the beginning of this essay, in order to see that the essential elements of the attitude which was there called the spirit of capitalism are the same as what we have just shown to be the content of the Puritan

---

[12] I make use of this opportunity to insert a few anti-critical remarks in advance of the main argument. Sombart *(Bourgeois)* makes the untenable statement that this ethic of Franklin is a word-for-word repetition of some writings of that great and versatile genius of the Renaissance, Leon Battista Alberti, who besides theoretical treatises on Mathematics, Sculpture, Painting, Architecture, and Love (he was personally a woman-hater), wrote a work in four books on household management (*Della Famiglia*). (Unfortunately, I have not at the time of writing been able to procure the edition of Mancini, but only the older one of Bonucci.) The passage from Franklin is printed above word for word. Where then are corresponding passages to be found in Alberti's work, especially the maxim "time is money", which stands at the head, and the exhortations which follow it? The only passage which, so far as I know, bears the slightest resemblance to it is found towards the end of the first book of *Della Famiglia* (ed. Bonucci, II, p. 353), where Alberti speaks in very general terms of money as the *nervus rerum* of the household, which must hence be handled with special care, just as Cato spoke in *De Re Rustica*.

[13] Unfortunately Brentano (*op. cit.*) has thrown every kind of struggle for gain, whether peaceful of warlike, into one pot, and has then set up as the specific criterion of capitalistic (as contrasted, for instance, with feudal) profit-seeking, its acquisitiveness of *money* (instead of land). Any further differentiation, which alone could lead to a clear conception, he has not only refused to make, but has made against the concept of the sprit of (modern) capitalism which we have formed for our purposes, the (to me) incompressible objection that it already includes in its assumptions what is supposed to be proved.

worldly asceticism[14] only without the religious basis, which by Franklin's time had died away. The idea that modern labour has an ascetic character is of course not new. Limitation to specialized work, with a renunciation of the Faustian universality of man which it involves, is a condition of any valuable work in the modern world; hence deeds and renunciation inevitably condition each other today. This fundamentally ascetic trait of middle-class life, if it attempts to be a way of life at all, and not simply the absence of any, was what Goethe wanted to teach, at the height of his wisdom, in the *Wander-jahren*, and in the end which he gave to the life of his *Faust*.[15] For him the realization meant a renunciation, a departure from an age of full and beautiful humanity, which can no more be repeated in the course of our cultural development than can the flower of the Athenian culture of antiquity.

The Puritan wanted to work in a calling; we are forced to do so. For when asceticism was carried out of monastic cells into everyday life, and began to dominate worldly morality, it did its part in building the tremendous cosmos of the modern economic order. This order is now bound to the technical and economic conditions of machine production which to-day determine the lives of all the individuals who are born into this mechanism, not only those directly concerned with economic acquisition, with irresistible force. Perhaps it will so determine them until the last ton of fossilized coal is burnt. In Baxter's view the care for external goods should only lie on the shoulders of the "saint like a light cloak, which can be thrown aside at any moment."[16] But fate decreed that the cloak should become an iron cage.

Since asceticism undertook to remodel the world and to work out its ideals in the world, material goods have gained an increasing and finally an inexorable power over the lives of men as at no previous period in history. To-day the spirit of religious asceticism—whether finally, who knows?—has escaped from the cage. But victorious capitalism, since it rests on mechanical foundations, needs its support no longer. The rosy blush of its laughing heir, the Enlightenment,

---

[14]That those other elements, which have here not yet been traced to their religious roots, especially the idea that honesty is the best policy (Franklin's discussion of credit), are also of Puritan origin, must be proved in a somewhat different connection (see the following essay [not translated here]. Here I shall limit myself to repeating the following remark of J. A. Rowntree (*Quakerism, Past and Present*, pp. 95–6), to which E. Bernstein has called my attention: "Is it merely a coincidence, or is it a consequence, that the lofty profession of spirituality made by the Friends has gone hand in hand with shrewdness and tact in the transaction of mundane affairs? Real piety favours the success of a trader by insuring his integrity and fostering habits of prudence and forethought, important items in obtaining that standing and credit in the commercial world, which are requisites for the steady accumulation of wealth" (see the following essay). "Honest as a Huguenot" was as proverbial in the seventeenth century as the respect of law of the Dutch which Sir W. Temple admired, and, a century later, that of the English as compared with those Continental peoples that had not been through this ethical schooling.

[15]Well analysed in Bielschowsky's *Goethe*, II, chap. xviii. For the development of the scientific cosmos Windelband, at the end of his *Blütezeit der deutschen Philosophie* (Vol. II of the *Gesch. D. Neueren Philosophie*), has expressed a similar idea.

[16]*Saints' Everlasting Rest*, chap. xii.

seems also to be irretrievably fading, and the idea of duty in one's calling prowls about in our lives like the ghost of dead religious beliefs. Where the fulfilment of the calling cannot directly be related to the highest spiritual and cultural values, or when, on the other hand, it need not be felt simply as economic compulsion, the individual generally abandons the attempt to justify it at all. In the field of its highest development, in the United States, the pursuit of wealth, stripped of its religious and ethical meaning, tends to become associated with purely mundane passions, which often actually give it the character of sport.[17]

No one knows who will live in this cage in the future, or whether at the end of this tremendous development entirely new prophets will arise, or there will be a great rebirth of old ideas and ideals, or, if neither, mechanized petrification, embellished with a sort of convulsive self-importance. For of the last stage of this cultural development, it might well be truly said: "Specialists without spirit, sensualists without heart; this nullity imagines that it has attained a level of civilization never before achieved."

But this brings us to the world of judgments of value and of faith, with which this purely historical discussion need not be burdened. The next task would be rather to show the significance of ascetic rationalism, which has only been touched in the foregoing sketch, for the content of practical social ethics, thus for the types of organization and the functions of social groups from the conventicle to the State. Then its relations to humanistic rationalism,[18] its ideals of life and cultural influence; further to the development of philosophical and scientific empiricism, to technical development and to spiritual ideals would have to be analysed. Then its historical development from the mediæval beginnings of worldly asceticism to its dissolution into pure utilitarianism would have to be traced out through all the areas of ascetic religion. Only then could the quantitative cultural significance of ascetic Protestantism in its relation to the other plastic elements of modern culture be estimated.

Here we have only attempted to trace the fact and the direction of its influence to their motives in one, though a very important point. But it would also further be necessary to investigate how Protestant Asceticism was in turn influenced in its development and its character by the totality of social conditions, especially economic.[19] The modern man is in general, even with the best will,

[17]"Couldn't the old man be satisfied with his $75,000 a year and rest? No! The frontage of the store must be widened to 400 feet. Why? That beats everything, he says. In the evening when his wife and daughter read together, he wants to go to bed. Sundays he looks at the clock every five minutes to see when the day will be over—what a futile life!" In these terms the son-in-law (who had emigrated from Germany) of the leading dry-goods man of an Ohio city expressed his judgment of the latter, a judgment which would undoubtedly have seemed simply incomprehensible to the old man. A symptom of German lack of energy.

[18]This remark alone (unchanged since his criticism) might have shown Brentano *(op. cit.)* that I have never doubted its independent significance. That humanism was also not pure rationalism has lately again been strongly emphasized by Borinski in the *Abhandl. der Münchener Akad. der Wiss., 1919*.

[19]The academic oration of v. Below, *Die Ursachen der Reformation* (Freiburg, 1916), is not concerned with this problem, but with that of the Reformation in general, especially Luther. For the question dealt with here, especially the controversies which have grown out of this study, I may refer finally to the work of Hermelink, *Reformation und Gegenreformation*, which, however, is also primarily concerned with other problems.

unable to give religious ideas a significance for culture and national character which they deserve. But it is, of course, not my aim to substitute for a one-sided materialistic an equally one-sided spiritualistic causal interpretation of culture and of history. Each is equally possible,[20] but each, if it does not serve as the preparation, but as the conclusion of an investigation, accomplishes equally little in the interest of historical truth.[21]

[20] For the above sketch has deliberately taken up only the relations in which an influence of religious ideas on the material culture is really beyond doubt. It would have been easy to proceed beyond that to a regular construction which logically deduced everything characteristic of modern cultures from Protestant rationalism. But that sort of thing may be left to the type of dilettante who believes in the unity of the group mind and its reducibility to a single formula. Let it be remarked only that the period of capitalistic development lying before that which we have studied was everywhere in part determined by religious influences, both hindering and helping. Of what sort these were belongs in another chapter. Furthermore, whether, of the broader problems sketched above, one or another can be dealt with in the limits of this Journal [the essay first appeared in the *Archiv für Sozialwissenschaft und Sozialpolitik*—Translator's Note] is not certain in view of the problems to which it is devoted. On the other hand, to write heavy tomes, as thick as they would have to be in this case, and dependent on the work of others (theologians and historians), I have no great inclination (I have left these sentences unchanged).

[21] I should have thought that this sentence and the remarks and notes immediately preceding it would have sufficed to prevent any misunderstanding of what this study was meant to accomplish, and I find no occasion for adding anything. Instead of following up with an immediate continuation in terms of the above programme, I have, partly for fortuitous reasons, especially the appearance of Troeltsch's *Die Soziallehren der christlichen Kirchen und Gruppen*, which disposed of many things I should have had to investigate in a way in which I, not being a theologian, could not have done it; but partly also in order to correct the isolation of this study and to place it in relation to the whole or culture development, determined, first, to write down some comparative studies of the general historical relationship of religion and society. These follow. Before them is placed only a short essay in order to clear up the concept of sect used above, and at the same time to show the significance of the Puritan conception of the Church for the capitalistic spirit of modern times.

Emile Durkheim (1858–1917) is widely acknowledged as one of the founders of sociology for his groundbreaking work in social theory, methodology, and substantive areas such as suicide, religion, and labor. In the following selection from his first book, *The Division of Labor in Society*, Durkheim explores the notion of social solidarity, that is, how individuals and society are bound together. Durkheim asserts that modern societies maintain their cohesion through dependencies brought about by the division of labor, not the sameness of responsibilities and tasks found in traditional societies. Law is different in each of these societies as well, as traditional societies governed by mechanical solidarity rely on repressive law, while modern societies with organic solidarity are characterized by restitutive law.

The Division of Labor in Society

Emile Durkheim

This work had its origins in the question of the relations of the individual to social solidarity. Why does the individual, while becoming more autonomous, depend more upon society? How can he be at once more individual and more solidary? Certainly, these two movements, contradictory as they appear, develop in parallel fashion. This is the problem we are raising. It appeared to us that what resolves this apparent antinomy is a transformation of social solidarity due to the steadily growing development of the division of labor. . . .

. . . The division of labor is not of recent origin, but it was only at the end of the eighteenth century that social cognizance was taken of the principle, though, until then, unwitting submission had been rendered to it. To be sure, several thinkers from earliest times saw its importance;[1] but Adam Smith was the first to attempt a theory of it. Moreover, he adopted this phrase that social science later lent to biology.

Nowadays, the phenomenon has developed so generally it is obvious to all. We need have no further illusions about the tendencies of modern industry; it advances steadily towards powerful machines, towards great concentrations of forces and capital, and consequently to the extreme division of labor. Occupations are infinitely separated and specialized, not only inside the factories, but each product is itself a specialty dependent upon others. Adam Smith and John Stuart Mill still hoped that agriculture, at least, would be an exception to the rule, and they saw it as the last resort of small-scale industry. Although one must be careful not to generalize unduly in such matters, nevertheless it is hard to deny today that the principal branches of the agricultural industry are steadily being drawn into the general movement.[2] Finally, business itself is inge-

---

[1] Aristotle, *Nichomachean Ethics*, E, 1133a, 16.

[2] *Journal des Economistes*, November 1884, p. 211.

niously following and reflecting in all its shadings the infinite diversity of industrial enterprises; and, while this evolution is realizing itself with unpremeditated spontaneity, the economists, examining its causes and appreciating its results, far from condemning or opposing it, uphold it as necessary. They see in it the supreme law of human societies and the condition of their progress.

But the division of labor is not peculiar to the economic world; we can observe its growing influence in the most varied fields of society. The political, administrative, and judicial functions are growing more and more specialized. It is the same with the aesthetic and scientific functions. It is long since philosophy reigned as the science unique; it has been broken into a multitude of special disciplines each of which has its object, method, and thought. "Men working in the sciences have become increasingly more specialized."[3] . . .

. . . The social relations to which the division of labor gives birth have often been considered only in terms of exchange, but this misinterprets what such exchange implies and what results from it. It suggests two beings mutually dependent because they are each incomplete, and translates this mutual dependence outwardly. It is, then, only the superficial expression of an internal and very deep state. Precisely because this state is constant, it calls up a whole mechanism of images which function with a continuity that exchange does not possess. The image of the one who completes us becomes inseparable from ours, not only because it is frequently associated with ours, but particularly because it is the natural complement of it. It thus becomes an integral and permanent part of our conscience, to such a point that we can no longer separate ourselves from it and seek to increase its force. That is why we enjoy the society of the one it represents, since the presence of the object that it expresses, by making us actually perceive it, sets it off more. On the other hand, we will suffer from all circumstances which, like absence or death, may have as effect the barring of its return or the diminishing of its vivacity.

As short as this analysis is, it suffices to show that this mechanism is not identical with that which serves as a basis for sentiments of sympathy whose source is resemblance. Surely there can be no solidarity between others and us unless the image of others unites itself with ours. But when the union results from the resemblance of two images, it consists in an agglutination. The two representations become solidary because, being indistinct, totally or in part, they confound each other, and become no more than one, and they are solidary only in the measure which they confound themselves. On the contrary, in the case of the division of labor, they are outside each other and are linked only because they are distinct. Neither the sentiments nor the social relations which derive from these sentiments are the same in the two cases.

We are thus led to ask if the division of labor would not play the same role in more extensive groups, if, in contemporary societies where it has developed as we know, it would not have as its function the integration of the social body to assure unity. It is quite legitimate to suppose that the facts which we have just

[3] De Candolle, *Histoire des Sciences et des Savants*, 2nd ed., p. 263.

observed reproduce themselves here, but with greater amplitude, that great political societies can maintain themselves in equilibrium only thanks to the specialization of tasks, that the division of labor is the source, if not unique, at least principal, of social solidarity. Comte took this point of view. Of all sociologists, to our knowledge, he is the first to have recognized in the division of labor something other than a purely economic phenomenon. He saw in it "the most essential condition of social life," provided that one conceives it "in all its rational extent; that is to say, that one applies it to the totality of all our diverse operations of whatever kind, instead of attributing it, as is ordinarily done, to simple material usages." Considered in this light, he says, "it leads immediately to regarding not only individuals and classes, but also, in many respects, different peoples, as at once participating, following a definite path in a special degree, exactly determined, in a work, immense and communal, whose inevitable gradual development links actual cooperators to their predecessors and even to their successors. It is thus the continuous repartition of different human endeavors which especially constitutes social solidarity and which becomes the elementary cause of the extension and growing complication of the social organism."[4]

If this hypothesis were proved, the division of labor would play a role much more important than that which we ordinarily attribute to it. It would serve not only to raise societies to luxury, desirable perhaps, but superfluous; it would be a condition of their existence. Through it, or at least particularly through it, their cohesion would be assured; it would determine the essential traits of their constitution. Accordingly, although we may not yet be in position to resolve the question rigorously, we can, however, imply from it now that, if such is really the function of the division of labor, it must have a moral character, for the need of order, harmony, and social solidarity is generally considered moral.

But before seeing whether this common opinion is well founded, we must verify the hypothesis that we have just given forth concerning the role of the division of labor. Let us see if, in effect, in the societies in which we live, it is from this that social solidarity essentially derives.

But how shall we proceed to such verification?

We must not simply look to see if, in these types of society, there exists a social solidarity which comes from the division of labor. That is a self-evident truism, since in such societies the division of labor is highly developed and produces solidarity. Rather we must especially determine in what degree the solidarity that it produces contributes to the general integration of society, for it is only then that we shall know how far necessary it is, whether it is an essential factor of social cohesion, or whether, on the contrary, it is only an accessory and secondary condition. To reply to this question, we must compare this social link to others in order to measure how much credit is due to it in the total effect; and to that end, we must begin by classifying the different types of social solidarity.

But social solidarity is a completely moral phenomenon which, taken by itself, does not lend itself to exact observation nor indeed to measurement. To

---

[4] Cours de philosophie positive, IV, p. 425.—Analogous ideas are found in Schaeffle, *Bau und Leben des sozialen Koerpers*, II, *passim*, and Clément, *Science Sociale*, I, pp. 235 ff.

proceed to this classification and this comparison, we must substitute for this internal fact which escapes us an external index which symbolizes it and study the former in the light of the latter.

This visible symbol is law. In effect, despite its immaterial character, wherever social solidarity exists, it resides not in a state of pure potentiality, but manifests its presence by sensible indices. Where it is strong, it leads men strongly to one another, frequently puts them in contact, multiplies the occasions when they find themselves related. To speak correctly, considering the point our investigation has reached, it is not easy to say whether social solidarity produces these phenomena, or whether it is a result of them, whether men relate themselves because it is a driving force, or whether it is a driving force because they relate themselves. However, it is not, at the moment, necessary to decide this question; it suffices to state that the two orders of fact are linked and vary at the same time and in the same sense. The more solidary the members of a society are, the more they sustain diverse relations, one with another, or with the group taken collectively, for, if their meetings were rare, they would depend upon one another only at rare intervals, and then tenuously. Moreover, the number of these relations is necessarily proportional to that of the juridical rules which determine them. Indeed, social life, especially where it exists durably, tends inevitably to assume a definite form and to organize itself, and law is nothing else than this very organization in so far as it has greater stability and precision. The general life of society cannot extend its sway without juridical life extending its sway at the same time and in direct relation. We can thus be certain of finding reflected in law all the essential varieties of social solidarity. . . .

. . . Shall we go further and say that social solidarity does not completely manifest itself perceptibly, that these manifestations are only partial and imperfect, that behind law and custom there is an internal state whence it derives, and that in order to know it truly we must intuit it without intermediaries?—But we can know causes scientifically only by the effects that they produce, and in order to determine their nature, science chooses from these effects only the most objective and most easily measurable. Science studies heat through the variations in volume which changes in temperature produce in bodies, electricity through its physico-chemical effects, force through movement. Why should social solidarity be an exception?

What remains of it divested of social forms? What gives it its specific characters is the nature of the group whose unity it assures; that is why it varies according to social types. It is not the same in the family and in political societies; we are not attached to our country in the same fashion as the Roman was to his city or the German to his tribe. But since these differences relate themselves to social causes, we can understand them only with reference to the differences that the social effects of solidarity present. If, then, we neglect the latter, all the varieties become indiscernible and we can no longer perceive what is common to all of them, that is, the general tendency to sociability, a tendency which is always and everywhere the same and is special to no particular social type. But this residue is only an abstraction, for sociability in itself is nowhere found. What exists and really lives are the particular forms of solidarity, domestic solidarity, occupational solidarity, national solidarity, yesterday's, today's, etc. Each has its proper nature; consequently, these general remarks, in every case, give only a very incomplete explanation of a phenomenon, since they necessarily omit the concrete and the vital.

The study of solidarity thus grows out of sociology. It is a social fact we can know only through the intermediary of social effects. If so many moralists and psychologists have been able to treat the question without following this procedure, it has been by circumventing the difficulty. They have eliminated from the phenomenon all that is peculiarly social in order to retain only the psychological germ whence it developed. It is surely true that solidarity, while being a social fact of the first order, depends on the individual organism. In order to exist, it must be contained in our physical and psychic constitution. One can thus rigorously limit oneself to studying this aspect. But, in that case, one sees only the most indistinct and least special aspect. It is not even solidarity properly speaking, but rather what makes it possible.

Moreover, this abstract study would not be very fertile in results. For, in its dependence upon a state of simple disposition in our psychic nature, solidarity is much too indefinite to be comprehended easily. It is an intangible phenomenon which does not lend itself to observation. In order to assume a comprehensible form, certain social consequences must translate it overtly. Moreover, even in this indeterminate state, it depends upon social conditions which explain it and from which, consequently, it cannot be detached. That is why it is very rare that some sociological views do not find their way into these analyses of pure psychology. For example, we speak of the influence of the *gregarious state* on the formation of social sentiment in general[5]; or perhaps indicate in short compass the principal social relations on which sociability quite apparently depends.[6] Without doubt, these complementary considerations, introduced helter-skelter, with examples and following chance suggestions, will not suffice to elucidate very much of the social nature of solidarity. They show, at least, that the sociological point of view is incumbent even upon psychologists.

Our method has now been fully outlined. Since law reproduces the principal forms of social solidarity, we have only to classify the different types of law to find therefrom the different types of social solidarity which correspond to it. It is now probable that there is a type which symbolizes this special solidarity of which the division of labor is the cause. That found, it will suffice, in order to measure the part of the division of labor, to compare the number of juridical rules which express it with the total volume of law.

For this task, we cannot use the distinctions utilized by the jurisconsults. Created for practical purposes, they can be very useful from this point of view, but science cannot content itself with these empirical classifications and approximations. The most accepted is that which divides law into public and private; the first is for the regulation of the relations of the individual to the State, the second, of individuals among themselves. But when we try to get closer to these

5 Bain, *The Emotions and the Will*, pp. 131 ff.

6 Spencer, *Principles of Psychology*, Part VIII, ch. v.

terms, the line of demarcation which appeared so neat at the beginning fades away. All law is private in the sense that it is always about individuals who are present and acting; but so, too, all law is public, in the sense that it is a social function and that all individuals are, whatever their varying titles, functionaries of society. Marital functions, paternal, etc., are neither delimited nor organized in a manner different from ministerial and legislative functions, and it is not without reason that Roman law entitled tutelage *munus publicum*. What, moreover, is the State? Where does it begin and where does it end? We know how controversial the question is; it is not scientific to make a fundamental classification repose on a notion so obscure and so badly analyzed.

To proceed scientifically, we must find some characteristic which, while being essential to juridical phenomena, varies as they vary. Every precept of law can be defined as a rule of sanctioned conduct. Moreover, it is evident that sanctions change with the gravity attributed to precepts, the place they hold in the public conscience, the role they play in society. It is right, then, to classify juridical rules according to the different sanctions which are attached to them.

They are of two kinds. Some consist essentially in suffering, or at least a loss, inflicted on the agent. They make demands on his fortune, or on his honor, or on his life, or on his liberty, and deprive him of something he enjoys. We call them repressive. They constitute penal law. It is true that those which are attached to rules which are purely moral have the same character, only they are distributed in a diffuse manner, by everybody indiscriminately, whereas those in penal law are applied through the intermediary of a definite organ; they are organized. As for the other type, it does not necessarily imply suffering for the agent, but consists only of *the return of things as they were,* in the reestablishment of troubled relations to their normal state, whether the incriminated act is restored by force to the type whence it deviated, or is annulled, that is, deprived of all social value. We must then separate juridical rules into two great classes, accordingly as they have organized repressive sanctions or only restitutive sanctions. The first comprise all penal law; the second, civil law, commercial law, procedural law, administrative and constitutional law, after abstraction of the penal rules which may be found there.

Let us now seek for the type of social solidarity to which each of these two types corresponds. . . .

. . . there exists a social solidarity which comes from a certain number of states of conscience which are common to all the members of the same society. This is what repressive law materially represents, at least in so far as it is essential. The part that it plays in the general integration of society evidently depends upon the greater or lesser extent of the social life which the common conscience embraces and regulates. The greater the diversity of relations wherein the latter makes its action felt, the more also it creates links which attach the individual to the group; the more, consequently, social cohesion derives completely from this source and bears its mark. But the number of these relations is itself proportional to that of the repressive rules. In determining what fraction of the juridical system penal law represents, we, at the same time, measure the relative importance of this solidarity. It is true that in such a procedure we do not take into account certain elements of the collective conscience which, because of their smaller power or their indeterminateness, remain foreign to repressive law while contributing to the assurance of social harmony. These are the ones protected by punishments which are merely diffuse. But the same is the case with other parts of law. There is not one of them which is not complemented by custom, and as there is no reason for supposing that the relation of law and custom is not the same in these different spheres, this elimination is not made at the risk of having to alter the results of our comparison. . . .

. . . the relations governed by co-operative law with restitutive sanctions and the solidarity which they express, result from the division of social labor. We have explained, moreover, that, in general, co-operative relations do not convey other sanctions. In fact, it is in the nature of special tasks to escape the action of the collective conscience, for, in order for a thing to be the object of common sentiments, the first condition is that it be common, that is to say, that it be present in all consciences and that all can represent it in one and the same manner. To be sure, in so far as functions have a certain generality, everybody can have some idea of them. But the more specialized they are, the more circumscribed the number of those cognizant of each of them. Consequently, the more marginal they are to the common conscience. The rules which determine them cannot have the superior force, the transcendent authority which, when offended, demands expiation. It is also from opinion that their authority comes, as is the case with penal rules, but from an opinion localized in restricted regions of society.

Moreover, even in the special circles where they apply and where, consequently, they are represented in people, they do not correspond to very active sentiments, nor even very often to any type of emotional state. For, as they fix the manner in which the different functions ought to concur in diverse combinations of circumstances which can arise, the objects to which they relate themselves are not always present to consciences. We do not always have to administer guardianship, trusteeship[7] or exercise the rights of creditor or buyer, etc., or even exercise them in such and such a condition. But the states of conscience are strong only in so far as they are permanent. The violation of these rules reaches neither the common soul of society in its living parts, nor even, at least not generally, that of special groups, and, consequently, it can determine only a very moderate reaction. All that is necessary is that the functions concur in a regular manner. If this regularity is disrupted, it behooves us to re-establish it. Assuredly, that is not to say that the development of the division of labor cannot be affective of penal law. There are, as we already know, administrative and governmental functions in which certain relations are regulated by repressive law, because of the particular character which the organ of common conscience and everything that relates to it has. In still other cases, the links of solidarity which unite certain social functions can be such that from their break quite general repercussions result invoking a penal sanction. But, for the reason we have given, these counter-blows are exceptional.

[7] That is why the law which governs the relations of domestic functions is not penal, although these functions are very general.

This law definitely plays a role in society analogous to that played by the nervous system in the organism. The latter has as its task, in effect, the regulation of the different functions of the body in such a way as to make them harmonize. It thus very naturally expresses the state of concentration at which the organism has arrived, in accordance with the division of physiological labor. Thus, on different levels of the animal scale, we can measure the degree of this concentration according to the development of the nervous system. Which is to say that we can equally measure the degree of concentration at which a society has arrived in accordance with the division of social labor according to the development of co-operative law with restitutive sanctions. We can foresee the great services that this criterion will render us.

Since negative solidarity does not produce any integration by itself, and since, moreover, there is nothing specific about it, we shall recognize only two kinds of positive solidarity which are distinguishable by the following qualities:

1. The first binds the individual directly to society without any intermediary. In the second, he depends upon society, because he depends upon the parts of which it is composed.
2. Society is not seen in the same aspect in the two cases. In the first, what we call society is a more or less organized totality of beliefs and sentiments common to all the members of the group: this is the collective type. On the other hand, the society in which we are solidary in the second instance is a system of different, special functions which definite relations unite. These two societies really make up only one. They are two aspects of one and the same reality, but none the less they must be distinguished.
3. From this second difference there arises another which helps us to characterize and name the two kinds of solidarity.

The first can be strong only if the ideas and tendencies common to all the members of the society are greater in number and intensity than those which pertain personally to each member. It is as much stronger as the excess is more considerable. But what makes our personality is how much of our own individual qualities we have, what distinguishes us from others. This solidarity can grow only in inverse ratio to personality. There are in each of us, as we have said, two consciences: one which is common to our group in its entirety, which, consequently, is not ourself, but society living and acting within us; the other, on the contrary, represents that in us which is personal and distinct, that which makes us an individual.[8] Solidarity which comes from likenesses is at its maximum when the collective conscience completely envelops our whole conscience and coincides in all points with it. But, at that moment, our individuality is nil. It can be born only if the community takes smaller toll of us. There are, here, two contrary forces, one centripetal, the other centrifugal, which cannot flourish at the same time. We cannot, at one and the same time, develop ourselves in two oppo-

[8] However, these two consciences are not in regions geographically distinct from us, but penetrate from all sides.

site senses. If we have a lively desire to think and act for ourselves, we cannot be strongly inclined to think and act as others do. If our ideal is to present a singular and personal appearance, we do not want to resemble everybody else. Moreover, at the moment when this solidarity exercises its force, our personality vanishes, as our definition permits us to say, for we are no longer ourselves, but the collective life.

The social molecules which can be coherent in this way can act together only in the measure that they have no actions of their own, as the molecules of inorganic bodies. That is why we propose to call this type of solidarity mechanical. The term does not signify that it is produced by mechanical and artificial means. We call it that only by analogy to the cohesion which unites the elements of an inanimate body, as opposed to that which makes a unity out of the elements of a living body. What justifies this term is that the link which thus unites the individual to society is wholly analogous to that which attaches a thing to a person. The individual conscience, considered in this light, is a simple dependent upon the collective type and follows all of its movements, as the possessed object follows those of its owner. In societies where this type of solidarity is highly developed, the individual does not appear, as we shall see later. Individuality is something which the society possesses. Thus, in these social types, personal rights are not yet distinguished from real rights.

It is quite otherwise with the solidarity which the division of labor produces. Whereas the previous type implies that individuals resemble each other, this type presumes their difference. The first is possible only in so far as the individual personality is absorbed into the collective personality; the second is possible only if each one has a sphere of action which is peculiar to him; that is, a personality. It is necessary, then, that the collective conscience leave open a part of the individual conscience in order that special functions may be established there, functions which it cannot regulate. The more this region is extended, the stronger is the cohesion which results from this solidarity. In effect, on the one hand, each one depends as much more strictly on society as labor is more divided; and, on the other, the activity of each is as much more personal as it is more specialized. Doubtless, as circumscribed as it is, it is never completely original. Even in the exercise of our occupation, we conform to usages, to practices which are common to our whole professional brotherhood. But, even in this instance, the yoke that we submit to is much less heavy than when society completely controls us, and it leaves much more place open for the free play of our initiative. Here, then, the individuality of all grows at the same time as that of its parts. Society becomes more capable of collective movement, at the same time that each of its elements has more freedom of movement. This solidarity resembles that which we observe among the higher animals. Each organ, in effect, has its special physiognomy, its autonomy. And, moreover, the unity of the organism is as great as the individuation of the parts is more marked. Because of this analogy, we propose to call the solidarity which is due to the division of labor, organic.

At the same time, this chapter and the preceding furnish us with the means to calculate the part which remains to each of these two social links in the total common result which they concur in producing through their different media. We know under what external forms these two types of solidarity are symbolized, that is to say, what the body of juridical rules which corresponds to each of them is. Consequently, in order to recognize their respective importance in a given social type, it is enough to compare the respective extent of the two types of law which express them, since law always varies as the social relations which it governs. . . .

. . . Not only, in a general way, does mechanical solidarity link men less strongly than organic solidarity, but also, as we advance in the scale of social evolution, it grows ever slacker.

The force of social links which have this origin vary with respect to the three following conditions:

1. The relation between the volume of the common conscience and that of the individual conscience. The links are as strong as the first more completely envelops the second.
2. The average intensity of the states of the collective conscience. The relation between volumes being equal, it has as much power over the individual as it has vitality. If, on the other hand, it consists of only feeble forces, it can but feebly influence the collective sense. It will the more easily be able to pursue its own course, and solidarity will be less strong.
3. The greater or lesser determination of these same states. That is, the more defined beliefs and practices are, the less place they leave for individual divergencies. They are uniform moulds into which we all, in the same manner, couch our ideas and our actions. The *consensus* is then as perfect as possible; all consciences vibrate in unison. Inversely, the more general and indeterminate the rules of conduct and thought are, the more individual reflection must intervene to apply them to particular cases. But it cannot awaken without upheavals occurring, for, as it varies from one man to another in quality and quantity, everything that it produces has the same character. Centrifugal tendencies thus multiply at the expense of social cohesion and the harmony of its movements.

On the other hand, strong and defined states of the common conscience are the roots of penal law. But we are going to see that the number of these is less today than heretofore, and that it diminishes, progressively, as societies approach our social type. It is thus that the average intensity and the mean degree of determination of collective states have themselves diminished. From this fact, it is true, we cannot conclude that the total extent of the common conscience has narrowed, for it may be that the region to which penal law corresponds has contracted, and that the remainder have dilated. It can have fewer strong and defined states, and retaliate with a very great number of others. But this growth, if it is real, is altogether equivalent to that which is produced in the individual conscience, for the latter has, at least, grown in the same proportions. If there are more things common to all, there are many more that are personal to each. There is, indeed, every reason for believing that the latter have increased more than the former, for the differences between men have become more pronounced in so far as they are more cultivated. We have just seen that special activities are more developed than the common conscience. It is, therefore, at least probable that, in each particular conscience, the personal sphere is much greater than the other. In any case, the relation between them has at most remained the same. Consequently, from this point of view, mechanical solidarity has gained nothing, even if it has not lost anything. If, on the other hand, we discover that the collective conscience has become more feeble and vaguer, we can rest assured that there has been an enfeeblement of this solidarity, since, in respect of the three conditions upon which its power of action rests, two, at least, are losing their intensity, while the third remains unchanged.

To prove this, it would avail us nothing to compare the number of rules with repressive sanctions in different social types, for the number of rules does not vary exactly with the sentiments the rules represent. The same sentiment can, in effect, be offended in several different ways, and thus give rise to several rules without diversifying itself in so doing. Because there are now more ways of acquiring property, there are also more ways of stealing, but the sentiment of respect for the property of another has not multiplied itself proportionally. . .

W.E.B. Du Bois (1868–1963) was a scholar, activist, and public intellectual who tirelessly pursued the study of race and racism in the United States. Du Bois held several different faculty positions, edited the NAACP's journal *Crisis*, and wrote numerous books, including the highly regarded *The Philadelphia Negro*. In the following selection from his book *The Souls of Black Folk*, Du Bois introduces the idea of the "double consciousness," where African-American identity is black on the one hand and American on the other, thus leaving "two souls, two thoughts, two unreconciled strivings. . . ." The concept of double consciousness has not only influenced contemporary sociology, but the field of literary studies as well.

The Souls of Black Folk

W.E.B. Du Bois

Of Our Spiritual Strivings

O water, voice of my heart, crying in the sand,
All night long crying with a mournful cry,
As I lie and listen, and cannot understand
The voice of my heart in my side or the voice of the sea,
O water, crying for rest, is it I, is it I?
All night long the water is crying to me.

Unresting water, there shall never be rest
Till the last moon droop and the last tide fail,
And the fire of the end begin to burn in the west;
And the heart shall be weary and wonder and cry like the sea,
All life long crying without avail,
As the water all night long is crying to me.

Arthur Symons

Between me and the other world there is ever an unasked question: unasked by some through feelings of delicacy; by others through the difficulty of rightly framing it. All, nevertheless, flutter round it. They approach me in a half-hesitant sort of way, eye me curiously or compassionately, and then, instead of saying directly, How does it feel to be a problem? they say, I know an excellent colored man in my town; or, I fought at Mechanicsville; or, Do not these Southern outrages make your blood boil? At these I smile, or am interested, or reduce the boiling to a simmer, as the occasion may require. To the real question, How does it feel to be a problem? I answer seldom a word.

And yet, being a problem is a strange experience,—peculiar even for one who has never been anything else, save perhaps in babyhood and in Europe. It is in the early days of rollicking boyhood that the revelation first bursts upon one, all in a day, as it were. I remember well when the shadow swept across me.

I was a little thing, away up in the hills of New England, where the dark Housatonic winds between Hoosac and Taghkanic to the sea. In a wee wooden schoolhouse, something put it into the boys' and girls' heads to buy gorgeous visiting-cards—ten cents a package—and exchange. The exchange was merry, till one girl, a tall newcomer, refused my card,—refused it peremptorily, with a glance. Then it dawned upon me with a certain suddenness that I was different from the others; or like, mayhap, in heart and life and longing, but shut out from their world by a vast veil. I had thereafter no desire to tear down that veil, to creep through; I held all beyond it in common contempt, and lived above it in a region of blue sky and great wandering shadows. That sky was bluest when I could beat my mates at examination-time, or beat them at a foot-race, or even beat their stringy heads. Alas, with the years all this fine contempt began to fade; for the worlds I longed for, and all their dazzling opportunities, were theirs, not mine. But they should not keep these prizes, I said; some, all, I would wrest from them. Just how I would do it I could never decide: by reading law, by healing the sick, by telling the wonderful tales that swam in my head,—some way. With other black boys the strife was not so fiercely sunny: their youth shrunk into tasteless sycophancy, or into silent hatred of the pale world about them and mocking distrust of everything white; or wasted itself in a bitter cry, Why did God make me an outcast and a stranger in mine own house? The shades of the prison-house closed round about us all: walls strait and stubborn to the whitest, but relentlessly narrow, tall, and unscalable to sons of night who must plod darkly on in resignation, or beat unavailing palms against the stone, or steadily, half hopelessly, watch the streak of blue above.

After the Egyptian and Indian, the Greek and Roman, the Teuton and Mongolian, the Negro is a sort of seventh son, born with a veil, and gifted with second-sight in this American world,—a world which yields him no true self-consciousness, but only lets him see himself through the revelation of the other world. It is a peculiar sensation, this double-consciousness, this sense of always looking at one's self through the eyes of others, of measuring one's soul by the tape of a world that looks on in amused contempt and pity. One ever feels his two-ness,—an American, a Negro; two souls, two thoughts, two unreconciled strivings; two warring ideals in one dark body, whose dogged strength alone keeps it from being torn asunder.

The history of the American Negro is the history of this strife,—this longing to attain self-conscious manhood, to merge his double self into a better and truer self. In this merging he wishes neither of the older selves to be lost. He would not Africanize America, for America has too much to teach the world and Africa. He would not bleach his Negro soul in a flood of white Americanism, for he knows that Negro blood has a message for the world. He simply wishes to make it possible for a man to be both a Negro and an American, without being cursed and spit upon by his fellows, without having the doors of Opportunity closed roughly in his face.

This, then, is the end of his striving: to be a co-worker in the kingdom of culture, to escape both death and isolation, to husband and use his best powers and his latent genius. These powers of body and mind have in the past been strangely wasted, dispersed, or forgotten. The shadow of a mighty Negro past flits through the tale of Ethiopia the Shadowy and of Egypt the Sphinx. Throughout history, the powers of single black men flash here and there like falling stars, and die sometimes before the world has rightly gauged their brightness. Here in America, in the few days since Emancipation, the black man's turning hither and thither in hesitant and doubtful striving has often made his very strength to lose effectiveness, to seem like absence of power, like weakness. And yet it is not weakness,—it is the contradiction of double aims. The double-aimed struggle of the black artisan—on the one hand to escape white contempt for a nation of mere hewers of wood and drawers of water, and on the other hand to plough and nail and dig for a poverty-stricken horde—could only result in making him a poor craftsman, for he had but half a heart in either cause. By the poverty and ignorance of his people, the Negro minister or doctor was tempted toward quackery and demagogy; and by the criticism of the other world, toward ideals that made him ashamed of his lowly tasks. The would-be black savant was confronted by the paradox that the knowledge his people needed was a twice-told tale to his white neighbors, while the knowledge which would teach the white world was Greek to his own flesh and blood. The innate love of harmony and beauty that set the ruder souls of his people a-dancing and a-singing raised but confusion and doubt in the soul of the black artist; for the beauty revealed to him was the soul-beauty of a race which his larger audience despised, and he could not articulate the message of another people. This waste of double aims, this seeking to satisfy two unreconciled ideals, has wrought sad havoc with the courage and faith and deeds of ten thousand thousand people,—has sent them often wooing false gods and invoking false means of salvation, and at times has even seemed about to make them ashamed of themselves.

Away back in the days of bondage they thought to see in one divine event the end of all doubt and disappointment; few men ever worshipped Freedom with half such unquestioning faith as did the American Negro for two centuries. To him, so far as he thought and dreamed, slavery was indeed the sum of all villainies, the cause of all sorrow, the root of all prejudice; Emancipation was the key to a promised land of sweeter beauty than ever stretched before the eyes of wearied Israelites. In song and exhortation swelled one refrain—Liberty; in his tears and curses the God he implored had Freedom in his right hand. At last it came,—suddenly, fearfully, like a dream. With one wild carnival of blood and passion came the message in his own plaintive cadences: —

> "Shout, O children!
> Shout, you're free!
> For God has bought your liberty!"

Years have passed away since then,—ten, twenty, forty; forty years of national life, forty years of renewal and development, and yet the swarthy spectre sits in its accustomed seat at the Nation's feast. In vain do we cry to this our vastest social problem: —

"Take any shape but that, and my firm nerves
Shall never tremble!"

The Nation has not yet found peace from its sins; the freedman has not yet found in freedom his promised land. Whatever of good may have come in these years of change, the shadow of a deep disappointment rests upon the Negro people,—a disappointment all the more bitter because the unattained ideal was unbounded save by the simple ignorance of a lowly people.

The first decade was merely a prolongation of the vain search for freedom, the boon that seemed ever barely to elude their grasp,—like a tantalizing will-o'-the-wisp, maddening and misleading the headless host. The holocaust of war, the terrors of the Ku-Klux Klan, the lies of carpet-baggers, the disorganization of industry, and the contradictory advice of friends and foes, left the bewildered serf with no new watchword beyond the old cry for freedom. As the time flew, however, he began to grasp a new idea. The ideal of liberty demanded for its attainment powerful means, and these the Fifteenth Amendment gave him. The ballot, which before he had looked upon as a visible sign of freedom, he now regarded as the chief means of gaining and perfecting the liberty with which war had partially endowed him. And why not? Had not votes made war and emancipated millions? Had not votes enfranchised the freedmen? Was anything impossible to a power that had done all this? A million black men started with renewed zeal to vote themselves into the kingdom. So the decade flew away, the revolution of 1876 came, and left the half-free serf weary, wondering, but still inspired. Slowly but steadily, in the following years, a new vision began gradually to replace the dream of political power,—a powerful movement, the rise of another ideal to guide the unguided, another pillar of fire by night after a clouded day. It was the ideal of "book-learning"; the curiosity, born of compulsory ignorance, to know and test the power of the cabalistic letters of the white man, the longing to know. Here at last seemed to have been discovered the mountain path to Canaan; longer than the highway of Emancipation and law, steep and rugged, but straight, leading to heights high enough to overlook life.

Up the new path the advance guard toiled, slowly heavily, doggedly; only those who have watched and guided the faltering feet, the misty minds, the dull understandings, of the dark pupils of these schools know how faithfully, how piteously, this people strove to learn. It was weary work. The cold statistician wrote down the inches of progress here and there, noted also where here and there a foot had slipped or some one had fallen. To the tired climbers, the horizon was ever dark, the mists were often cold, the Canaan was always dim and far away. If, however, the vistas disclosed as yet no goal, no resting-place, little but flattery and criticism, the journey at least gave leisure for reflection and self-examination; it changed the child of Emancipation to the youth with dawning self-consciousness, self-realization, self-respect. In those sombre forests of his striving his own soul rose before him, and he saw himself,—darkly as through a veil; and yet he saw in himself some faint revelation of his power, of his mission. He began to have a dim feeling that, to attain his place in the world, he must be himself, and not another. For the first time he sought to analyze the burden he bore upon his back, that dead-weight of social degradation partially masked behind a half-named Negro problem. He felt his poverty; without a cent, without a home, without land, tools, or savings, he had entered into competition with rich, landed, skilled neighbors. To be a poor man is hard, but to be a poor race in a land of dollars is the very bottom of hardships. He felt the weight of his ignorance,—not simply of letters, but of life, of business, of the humanities; the accumulated sloth and shirking and awkwardness of decades and centuries shackled his hands and feet. Nor was his burden all poverty and ignorance. The red stain of bastardy, which two centuries of systematic legal defilement of Negro women had stamped upon his race, meant not only the loss of ancient African chastity, but also the hereditary weight of a mass of corruption from white adulterers, threatening almost the obliteration of the Negro home.

A people thus handicapped ought not to be asked to race with the world, but rather allowed to give all its time and thought to its own social problems. But alas! while sociologists gleefully count his bastards and his prostitutes, the very soul of the toiling, sweating black man is darkened by the shadow of a vast despair. Men call the shadow prejudice, and learnedly explain it as the natural defence of culture against barbarism, learning against ignorance, purity against crime, the "higher" against the "lower" races. To which the Negro cries Amen! and swears that to so much of this strange prejudice as is founded on just homage to civilization, culture, righteousness, and progress, he humbly bows and meekly does obeisance. But before that nameless prejudice that leaps beyond all this he stands helpless, dismayed, and well-nigh speechless; before that personal disrespect and mockery, the ridicule and systematic humiliation, the distortion of fact and wanton license of fancy, the cynical ignoring of the better and the boisterous welcoming of the worse, the all-pervading desire to inculcate disdain for everything black, from Toussaint to the devil,—before this there rises a sickening despair that would disarm and discourage any nation save that black host to whom "discouragement" is an unwritten word.

But the facing of so vast a prejudice could not but bring the inevitable self-questioning, self-disparagement, and lowering of ideals which ever accompany repression and breed in an atmosphere of contempt and hate. Whisperings and portents came borne upon the four winds: Lo! we are diseased and dying, cried the dark hosts; we cannot write, our voting is vain; what need of education, since we must always cook and serve? And the Nation echoed and enforced this self-criticism, saying: Be content to be servants, and nothing more; what need of higher culture for half-men? Away with the black man's ballot, by force or fraud,—and behold the suicide of a race! Nevertheless, out of the evil came something of good,—the more careful adjustment of education to real life, the clearer perception of the Negroes' social responsibilities, and the sobering realization of the meaning of progress.

So dawned the time of *Sturm und Drang*: storm and stress to-day rocks our little boat on the mad waters of the world-sea; there is within and without the sound of conflict, the burning of body and rending of soul; inspiration strives with doubt, and faith with vain questionings. The bright ideals of the past,—physical freedom, political power, the training of brains and the training of hands,—all these in turn have waxed and waned, until even the last grows dim and overcast. Are they all wrong,—all false? No, not that, but each alone was over-simple and incomplete,—the dreams of a credulous race-childhood, or the fond imaginings of the other world which does not know and does not want to know our power. To be really true, all these ideals must be melted and welded into one. The training of the schools we need to-day more than ever,—the training of deft hands, quick eyes and ears, and above all the broader, deeper, higher culture of gifted minds and pure hearts. The power of the ballot we need in sheer self-defence,—else what shall save us from a second slavery? Freedom, too, the long-sought, we still seek,—the freedom of life and limb, the freedom to work and think, the freedom to love and aspire. Work, culture, liberty,—all these we need, not singly but together, not successively but together, each growing and aiding each, and all striving toward that vaster ideal that swims before the Negro people, the ideal of human brotherhood, gained through the unifying ideal of Race; the ideal of fostering and developing the traits and talents of the Negro, not in opposition to or contempt for other races, but rather in large conformity to the greater ideals of the American Republic, in order that some day on American soil two world-races may give each to each those characteristics both so sadly lack. We the darker ones come even now not altogether empty-handed: there are to-day no truer exponents of the pure human spirit of the Declaration of Independence than the American Negroes; there is no true American music but the wild sweet melodies of the Negro slave; the American fairy tales and folk-lore are Indian and African; and, all in all, we black men seem the sole oasis of simple faith and reverence in a dusty desert of dollars and smartness. Will America be poorer if she replace her brutal dyspeptic blundering with light-hearted but determined Negro humility? or her coarse and cruel wit with loving jovial good-humor? or her vulgar music with the soul of the Sorrow Songs?

Merely a concrete test of the underlying principles of the great republic is the Negro Problem, and the spiritual striving of the freedmen's sons is the travail of souls whose burden is almost beyond the measure of their strength, but who bear it in the name of an historic race, in the name of this the land of their fathers' fathers, and in the name of human opportunity.

Harriet Martineau (1802–1876) has been called the "first woman sociologist." Although perhaps best known for her translation of August Comte's *Cours de philosophie positive* into English, Martineau made important but sometimes overlooked contributions to social science methodology and comparative sociology. *Society in America*, the book from which the following contribution is drawn, is a wide ranging treatise based on Martineau's observations of the expression of nineteenth century American values and morality. Martineau strongly opposed racial and gender inequality and sought to understand how a society that claimed to value freedom and equality in principle was so discriminatory and exclusionary in practice.

SOCIETY IN AMERICA

Harriet Martineau

In seeking for methods by which I might communicate what I have observed in my travels, without offering any pretension to teach the English, or judge the Americans, two expedients occurred to me; both of which I have adopted. One is, to compare the existing state of society in America with the principles on which it is professedly founded; thus testing Institutions, Morals, and Manners by an indisputable, instead of an arbitrary standard, and securing to myself the same point of view with my readers of both nations.

In working according to this method, my principal dangers are two. I am in danger of not fully apprehending the principles on which society in the United States is founded; and of erring in the application of these of the facts which came under my notice. In the last respect, I am utterly hopeless of my own accuracy. It is in the highest degree improbable that my scanty gleanings in the wide field of American society should present a precisely fair sample of the whole. I can only explain that I have spared no pains to discover the truth, in both divisions of my task; and invite correction, in all errors of fact. This I earnestly do; holding myself, of course, an equal judge with others on maters of opinion.

My readers, on their part, will bear in mind that, in showing discrepancies between an actual condition and a pure and noble theory of society, I am not finding fault with the Americans, as falling behind the English, or the French, or any other nation. I decline the office of censor altogether. I dare not undertake it. Nor will my readers, I trust, regard the subject otherwise than as a compound of philosophy and fact. If we can all, for once, allay our personal feelings, dismiss our too great regard to mutual opinion, and put praise and blame as nearly as possible out of the question, more that is advantageous to us may perhaps be learned than by any invidious comparisons and proud judgments that were ever instituted and pronounced.

The other method by which I propose to lessen my own responsibility, is to enable my readers to judge for themselves, better than I can for them, what my testimony is worth. For this purpose, I offer a brief account of my travels, with dates in full; and a report of the principal means I enjoyed of obtaining a knowledge of the country. . .

. . . In the course of this tour, I visited almost every kind of institution. The prisons of Auburn, Philadelphia, and Nashville: the insane and other hospitals of almost every considerable place: the literary and scientific institutions; the factories of the north; the plantations of the south; the farms of the west. I lived in houses which might be called palaces, in log-houses, and in a farm-house. I traveled much in wagons, as well as stages; also on horseback, and in some of the best and worst of steamboats. I saw weddings, and christenings; the gatherings of the richer at watering places, and the humbler at country festivals. I was present at orations, at land sales, and in the slave market. I was in frequent attendance on the Supreme Court and the Senate; and witnessed some of the proceedings of state legislatures. Above all, I was received into the bosom of many families, not as a stranger, but as a daughter or a sister. I am qualified, if any one is, to testify to the virtues and the peace of the homes of the United States; and let it not be thought a breach of confidence, if I should be found occasionally to have spoken of these out of the fullness of my heart.

It would be nearly impossible to relate whom I knew, during my travels. Nearly every eminent man in politics, science and literature, and almost every distinguished woman, would grace my list. I have respected and beloved friends of each political party; and of nearly every religious denomination; among slave-holders, colonizationists, and abolitionists; among farmers, lawyers, merchants, professors, and clergy. I traveled among several tribes of Indians; and spent months in the southern States, with negroes ever at my heels.

Such were my means of information. . .

Morals of Slavery

This title is not written down in a spirit of mockery; though there appears to be a mockery somewhere, when we contrast slavery with the principles and the rule which are the test of all American institutions:—the principles that all men are born free and equal; that rulers derive their just powers from the consent of the governed; and the rule of reciprocal justice. This discrepancy between principles and practice needs no more words. But the institution of slavery exists; and what we have to see is what the morals are of the society which is subject to it.

What social virtues are possible in a society of which injustice is the primary characteristic? In a society which is divided into two classes, the servile and the imperious?

The most obvious is Mercy. Nowhere, perhaps, can more touching exercises of mercy be seen than here. It must be remembered that the greater number of slave-holders have no other idea than of holding slaves. Their fathers did it: they themselves have never known the coloured race treated otherwise than as inferior beings, born to work for and to teaze the whites; helpless, improvident, open to no higher inducements than indulgence and praise; capable of nothing but entire dependence. The good affections of slave-holders like these show themselves in the form of mercy; which is as beautiful to witness as mercy, made a substitute for justice, can ever be. I saw endless manifestations of mercy, as well as of its opposite. The thoughtfulness of masters, mistresses, and their children about, not only the comforts, but the indulgences of their slaves, was a frequent subject of admiration with me. Kind masters are liberal in the expenditure of money, and (what is better) of thought, in gratifying the whims and fancies of their negroes. They make large sacrifices occasionally for the social or domestic advantage of their people; and use great forbearance in the exercise of the power conferred upon them by law and custom.

Nothing struck me more than the patience of slave-owners. In this virtue they probably surpass the whole Christian world;—I mean in their patience with their slaves; for one cannot much praise their patience with the abolitionists, or with the tariff; or in some other cases of political vexation. When I considered how they love to be called "fiery southerners," I could not but marvel at their mild forbearance under the hourly provocations to which they are liable in their homes. It is found that such a degree of this virtue can be obtained only by long habit. Persons from New England, France, or England, becoming slave-holders, are found to be the most severe masters and mistresses, however good their tempers may always have appeared previously. They cannot, like the native proprietor, sit waiting half an hour for the second course, or see everything done in the worst possible manner; their rooms dirty, their property wasted, their plans frustrated, their infants slighted, themselves deluded by artifices,—they cannot, like the native proprietor, endure all this unruffled. It seems to me that every slave-holder's temper is subjected to a discipline which must either ruin or perfect it. While we know that many tempers are thus ruined, and must mourn for the unhappy creatures who cannot escape from their tyranny, it is evident, on the other hand, that many tempers are to be met with which should shame down and silence for ever the irritability of some whose daily life is passed under circumstances of comparative ease.

This mercy, indulgence, patience, was often pleaded to me in defense of the system, or in aggravation of the faults of intractable slaves. The fallacy of this is so gross as not to need exposure anywhere but on the spot. I was heart-sick of being told of the ingratitude of slaves, and wary of explaining that indulgence can never atone for injury: that the extremest pampering, for a life-time, is no equivalent for rights withheld, no reparation for irreparable injustice. What are the greatest possible amounts of finery, sweetmeats, dances, gratitudes, and kind words and looks, in exchange for political, social, and domestic existence? For body and spirit? Is it not true that the life is more than meat, and the body than raiment? . . .

. . . A common question put to me by amiable ladies was, "Do not you find the slaves generally very happy?" They never seemed to have been asked, or to have asked themselves, the question with which I replied:—"Would you be happy with their means?" . . .

. . . Of course, in a society where things like these are said and done by its choicest members, there is a prevalent unconsciousness of the existing wrong. The daily and hourly plea is of good intentions towards the slaves; of innocence under the aspersions of foreigners. They are as sincere in the belief that they are injured as their visitors are cordial in their detestation of the morals of slavery. Such unconsciousness of the milder degrees of impurity and injustice as enables ladies and clergymen of the highest character to speak and act as I have related, is a sufficient evidence of the prevalent grossness of morals. One remarkable indication of such blindness was the almost universal mention of the state of the Irish to me, as a worse case than American slavery. I never attempted, of course, to vindicate the state of Ireland: but I was surprised to find no one able, till put in the way, to see the distinction between political misgovernment and personal slavery: between exasperating a people by political insult, and possessing them, like brutes, for pecuniary profit. The unconsciousness of guilt is the worst of symptoms, where there are means of light to be had.

The degradation of the women is so obvious a consequence of the evils disclosed above, that the painful subject need not be enlarged on. By the degradation of women, I do not mean to imply any doubt of the purity of their manners. There are reasons, plain enough to the observer, why their manners should be even peculiarly pure. They are all married young, from their being out-numbered by the other sex: and there is ever present an unfortunate servile class of their own sex to serve the purpose of licentiousness, so as to leave them untempted. Their degradation arises, not from their own conduct, but from that of all other parties about them. Where the generality of men carry secrets which their wives must be the last to know; where the busiest and more engrossing concerns of life must wear one aspect to the one sex, and another to the other, there is an end to all wholesome confidence and sympathy, and woman sinks to be the ornament of her husband's house, the domestic manager of his establishment, instead of being his all-sufficient friend. I am speaking not only of what I suppose must necessarily be; but of what I have actually seen. I have seen, with heart-sorrow, the kind politeness, the gallantry, so insufficient to the loving heart, with which the wives of the south are treated by their husbands. I have seen the horror of a woman's having to work,—to exert the faculties which her Maker gave her;—the eagerness to ensure her unearned ease and rest; the deepest insult which can be offered to an intelligent and conscientious woman. I know the tone of conversation which is adopted towards women; different in its topics and its style from that which any man would dream of offering to any other man. I have heard the boast of the chivalrous consideration in which women are held throughout their woman's paradise; and seen something of the anguish of crushed pride, of the conflict of bitter feelings with which such boasts have been listened to by those whose aspirations teach them the hollowness of the system. The gentlemen are all the while unaware that women are not treated in the best possible manner among them: and they will remain thus blind as long as licentious intercourse with the lowest of the sex unfits them for appreciating the highest. A lady who, brought up elsewhere to use her own faculties, and employ them on such objects as she thinks proper, and who has more knowledge and more wisdom that perhaps any gentleman of her acquaintance, told me of the disgust with which she submits to the conversation which is addressed to her, under the idea of being fit for her; and how she solaces herself at home, after such provocation, with the silent sympathy of books. A father of promising young daughters, whom he sees likely to be crushed by the system, told me, in a tone of voice which I shall never forget, that women there might as well be turned into the street, for anything they are fit for. There are reasonable hopes that his children may prove an exception. One gentleman who declares himself much interested in the whole subject, expresses his horror of the employment of women in the northern States, for useful purposes. He told me that the same force of circumstances which, in the region he inhabits, makes me independent, increases the dependence of women, and will go on to increase it. Society is there, he declared, "always advancing toward orientalism."

Of course, the children suffer, perhaps the most fatally of all, under the slave system. What can be expected from little boys who are brought up to consider physical courage the highest attribute of manhood; pride of section and of caste its loftiest grace; the slavery of a part of society essential to the freedom of the rest; justice of less account than generosity; and humiliation in the eyes of men the most intolerable of evils? What is to be expected of little girls who boast of having got a negro flogged for being impertinent to them, and who are surprised at the "ungentlemanly" conduct of a master who maims his slave? Such lessons are not always taught expressly. Sometimes the reverse is expressly taught. But this is what the children in a slave country necessarily learn from what passes around them; just as the plainest girls in a school grow up to think personal beauty the most important of all endowments, in spite of daily assurances that the charms of the mind are all that are worth regarding.

The children of slave countries learn more and worse still. It is nearly impossible to keep them from close intercourse with the slaves; and the attempt is rarely made. The generality of slaves are as gross as the total absence of domestic sanctity might be expected to render them. They do not dream of any reserves with children. The consequences are inevitable.

One of the absolutely inevitable results of slavery is a disregard of human rights; an inability even to comprehend them. Probably the southern gentry, who declare that the presence of slavery enhances the love of freedom; that freedom can be duly estimated only where a particular class can appropriate all social privileges; that, to use the words of one of them, "they know too much of slavery to be slaves themselves," are sincere enough in such declarations; and if so, it follows that they do not know what freedom is. They may have the benefit of the alternative,—of not knowing what freedom is, and being sincere; or of knowing what freedom is, and not being sincere. I am disposed to think that the first is the more common case . . .

Women

If a test of civilization be sought, none can be so sure as the condition of that half of society over which the other half has power, —from the exercise of the right of the strongest. Tried by this test, the American civilization appears to be of a lower order than might have been expected from some other symptoms of its social state. The Americans have, in the treatment of women, fallen below, not only their own democratic principles, but the practice of some parts of the Old World.

The unconsciousness of both parties as to the injuries suffered by women at the hands of those who hold the power is a sufficient proof of the low degree of civilization in this important particular at which they rest. While woman's intellect is confined, her morals crushed, her health ruined, he weaknesses encouraged, and her strength punished, she is told that her lot is cast in the paradise of women: and there is no country in the world where there is so much boasting of the "chivalrous" treatment she enjoys. That is to say, —she has the best place in stagecoaches: when there are not chairs enough for everybody, the gentlemen stand: she hears oratorical flourishes on public occasions about wives and home, and apostrophes to woman: her husband's hair stands on end at the idea of her working, and he toils to indulge her with money: she has liberty to get her brain turned by religions excitements, that her attention may be diverted from morals, politics, and philosophy; and, especially her morals are guarded by the strictest observance of propriety in her presence. In short, indulgence is given her as a substitute for justice. Her case differs from that of the slave, as to the principle just so far as this; that the indulgence is large and universal, instead of petty and capricious. In both cases, justice is denied on no better plea that the right of the strongest. In both cases, the acquiescence of the many, and the burning discontent of the few, of the oppressed, testify, the one to the actual degradation of the class, and the other to its fitness for the enjoyment of human rights.

The intellect of woman is confined by an unjustifiable restriction of both methods of education,—by express teaching, and by the discipline of circumstance. The former, though prior in the chronology of each individual, is a direct consequence of the latter, as regards the whole of the sex. As women have none of the objects in life for which an enlarged education is considered requisite, the education is not given. Female education in America is much what it is in England. There is a profession of some things being taught which are supposed necessary because everybody learns them. They serve to fill up time, to occupy attention harmlessly, to improve conversation, and to make women something like companions to their husbands, and able to teach their children somewhat. But what is given is, for the most part, passively received; and what is obtained is, chiefly, by means of the memory. There is rarely or never a careful ordering of influences for the promotion of clear intellectual activity. Such activity, when it exceeds that which is necessary to make the work of the teacher easy, is feared and repressed. This is natural enough, as long as women are excluded from the objects for which men are trained. While there are natural rights which women may not use, just claims which are not to be listened to, large objects which may not be approached, even in imagination, intellectual activity is dangerous: or, as the phrase is, unfit. Accordingly, marriage is the only object left open to woman. Philosophy she may pursue only fancifully, and under pain of ridicule: science only as a pastime, and under a similar penalty. Art is declared to be left open: but the necessary learning, and, yet more, the indispensable experience of reality, are denied to her. Literature is also said to be permitted: but under what penalties and restrictions? Nothing is thus left for women but marriage.—Yes; Religion, is the reply.—Religion is a temper, not a pursuit. It is the moral atmosphere in which human beings are to live and move. Men do not live to breathe: they breathe to live.

The morals of women are crushed. If there be any human power and business and privilege which is absolutely universal, it is the discovery and adoption of the principle and laws of duty. As every individual, whether man or woman, has a reason and a conscience, this is a work which each is thereby authorized to do for him or herself. But it is not only virtually prohibited to beings who, like the American women, have scarcely any object in life proposed to them; but the whole apparatus of opinion is brought to bear offensively upon individuals among women who exercise freedom of mind in deciding upon what duty is, and the methods by which it is to be pursued. There is nothing extraordinary to the disinterested observer in women being so grieved at the case of slaves,—slave wives and mothers, as well as spirit-broken men,—as to wish to do what they could for their relief: there is nothing but what is natural in their being ashamed of the cowardice of such white slaves of the north as are deterred by intimidation from using their rights of speech and of the press, in behalf of the suffering race, and in their resolving not to do likewise: there is nothing but what is justifiable in their using their moral freedom, each for herself, in neglect of the threats of punishment: yet there were no bounds to the efforts made to crush the actions of woman who thus used their human powers in the abolition question, and the convictions of those who looked on, and who might possibly be warmed into free action by the beauty of what they saw. It will be remembered that they were women who asserted the right of meeting and of discussion, on the day when Garrison was mobbed in Boston. Bills were posed about the city on this occasion, denouncing these women as casting off the refinement and delicacy of their sex: the newspapers, which laud the exertions of ladies in all other charities for the prosecution of which they are wont to meet and speak, teemed with the most disgusting reproaches and insinuations: and the pamphlets which related to the question all presumed to censure the act of duty which the women had performed in deciding upon their duty for themselves.—One lady, of high talents and character, whose books were very popular before she did a deed greater than that of writing any book, in acting upon an unusual conviction of duty, and becoming an abolitionist, has been almost excommunicated since. A family of ladies, whose talent and conscientiousness had placed them high in the estimation of society as teachers, have lost all their pupils since they declared their anti-slavery opinions. The reproach in all the many similar cases that I know is, not that the ladies hole anti-slavery opinions, but that they act upon them.

How fearfully the morals of woman are crushed, appears from the prevalent persuasion that there are virtues which are peculiarly masculine, and others which are peculiarly feminine. It is not only that masculine and feminine employments are supposed to be properly different. No one in the world, I believe, questions this. But it is actually supposed that what are called the hardy virtues are more appropriate to men, and the gentler to women. As all virtues nourish each other, and can no otherwise be nourished, the consequence of the admitted fallacy is that men are, after all, not nearly so brave as they ought to be; nor women so gentle. But what is the manly character till it be gently? The very word magnanimity cannot be thought of in relation to it till it becomes mild—Christ-like. Again, what can a woman be, or do, without bravery? While woman is human, men should beware how they deprive her of any of the strength which is all needed for the strife and burden of humanity. Let them beware how they put her off her watch and defence, by promises which they cannot fulfil;—promises of a guardianship which can arise only from within; of support which can be derived only from the freest moral action,—from the self-reliance which can be generated by no other means.

But, it may be asked, how does society get on,—what does it do? For it acts on the supposition of there being masculine and feminine virtues,—upon the fallacy just exposed.

It does so; and the consequences are what might be looked for. Men are ungentle, tyrannical. They abuse the right of the strongest, however they may veil the abuse with indulgence. They want the magnanimity to discern woman's human rights; and they crush her morals rather than allow them. Women are, as might be anticipated, weak, ignorant and subservient, in as far as they exchange self-reliance for reliance on anything out of themselves. Those who will not submit to such a suspension of their moral functions, (for the work of self-perfection remains to be done, sooner or later,) have to suffer for their allegiance to duty. They have all the need of bravery that the few heroic men who assert the highest rights of women have of gentleness, to guard them from the encroachment to which power, custom, and education, incessantly conduce.

Such brave women and such just men there are in the United States, scattered among the multitude, whose false apprehension of rights leads to an enormous failure of duties. There are enough of such to commend the true understanding and practice to the simplest minds and most faithful hearts of the community, under whose testimony the right principle will spread and flourish. If it were not for the external prosperity of the country, the injured half of its society would probably obtain justice sooner than in any country of Europe. But the prosperity of America is a circumstance unfavourable to its women. It will be long before they are put to the proof as to what they are capable of thinking and doing: a proof to which hundreds, perhaps thousands of Englishwomen have been put by adversity, and the result of which is a remarkable improvement in their social condition, even within the space of ten years. Persecution for opinion, punishment for all manifestations of intellectual and moral strength, are still as common as women who have opinions and who manifest strength: but some things are easy, and many are possible of achievement, to women of ordinary powers, which it would have required genius to accomplish but a few years ago.

Jane Addams (1860–1935) made important contributions to applied sociology, peace studies, urban studies, and feminism. Perhaps best-known as the founder of Hull House in Chicago, Addams' sociology has not received the attention it deserves, although in recent years there has been increased appreciation of her path-breaking work in humanistic sociology and criminology. In the following excerpt, Addams offers a clever critique of patriarchy centered on the dynamics of gender roles in industry, education, and government.

If Men Were Seeking the Franchise

Jane Addams

Let us imagine throughout this article, if we can sustain an absurd hypothesis so long, the result upon society if the matriarchal period had held its own; if the development of the State had closely followed that of the family until the chief care of the former, as that of the latter, had come to be the nurture and education of children and the protection of the weak, sick and aged. In short let us imagine a hypothetical society organized upon the belief that "there is no wealth but life." With this Ruskinian foundation let us assume that the political machinery of such a society, the franchise and the rest of it, were in the hands of women because they had always best exercised those functions. Let us further imagine a given moment when these women, who in this hypothetical society had possessed political power from the very beginnings of the State, where being appealed to by the voteless men that men might be associated with women in the responsibilities of citizenship.

Plagiarizing somewhat upon recent suffrage speeches let us consider various replies which these citizen women might reasonably make to the men who were seeking the franchise; the men insisting that only through the use of the ballot could they share the duties of the State.

First, could not the women say: "Our most valid objection to extending the franchise to you is that you are so fond of fighting—you always have been since you were little boys. You'd very likely forget that the real object of the State is to nurture and protect life, and out of sheer vainglory you would be voting away huge sums of money for battleships, not one of which could last more than a few years, and yet each would cost ten million dollars; more money than all the buildings of Harvard University represent, although it is the richest educational institution in America. Every time a gun is fired in a battleship it expends, or rather explodes, seventeen hundred dollars, as much as a college education costs many a country boy, and yet you would be firing off these guns as mere salutes, with no enemy within three thousand miles, simply because you so enjoy the sound of shooting.

"Our educational needs are too great and serious to run any such risk. Democratic government itself is perilous unless the electorate is educated; our industries are suffering for lack of skilled workmen; more than half a million immigrants a year must be taught the underlying principles of republican government. Can we, the responsible voters, take the risk of wasting our taxes by extending the vote to those who have always been so ready to lose their heads over mere military display?"

Second, would not the hypothetical women, who would have been responsible for the advance of industry during these later centuries, as women actually were during the earlier centuries when they dragged home the game and transformed the pelts into shelter and clothing, say further to these disenfranchised men: "We have carefully built up a code of factory legislation for the protection of the workers in modern industry; we know that you men have always been careless about the house, perfectly indifferent to the necessity for sweeping and cleaning; if you were made responsible for factory legislation it is quite probable that you would let the workers in the textile mills contract tuberculosis through needlessly breathing the fluff, or the workers in machine shops through inhaling metal filings, both of which are now carried off by an excellent suction system which we women have insisted upon, but which it is almost impossible to have installed in a man-made State because the men think so little of dust and its evil effects. In many Nations in which political power is confined to men, and this is notably true in the United States of America, there is no protection even for the workers in white lead, although hundreds of them are yearly incapacitated from lead poisoning, and others actually die.

"We have also heard that in certain States, in order to save the paltry price of a guard which would protect a dangerous machine, men legislators allow careless boys and girls to lose their fingers and sometimes their hands, thereby crippling their entire futures. These male legislators do not make guarded machinery obligatory, although they know that when the heads of families are injured at these unprotected machines the State must care for them in hospitals, and when they are killed, that if necessary the State must provide for their widows and children in poorhouses."

These wise women, governing the State with the same care they had always put into the management of their families, would further place against these men seeking the franchise the charge that men do not really know how tender and delicate children are, and might therefore put them to work in factories, as indeed they have done in man-made States during the entire period of factory production. We can imagine these women saying: "We have been told that in certain States children are taken from their beds in the early morning before it is light and carried into cotton mills, where they are made to run back and forth tending the spinning frames until their immature little bodies are so bent and strained that they never regain their normal shapes; that little children are allowed to work in canneries for fifteen and seventeen hours until, utterly exhausted, they fall asleep among the debris of shells and husks."

Would not these responsible women voters gravely shake their heads and say that as long as men exalt business profit above human life it would be sheer folly to give them the franchise; that, of course, they would be slow to make such matters the subject of legislation?

Would not the enfranchised women furthermore say to these voteless men:

"You have always been so eager to make money; what assurance have we that in your desire to get the largest amount of coal out of the ground in the shortest possible time you would not permit the mine supports to decay and mine damp to accumulate until the percentage of accidents among miners would be simply heartbreaking? Then you are so reckless. Business seems to you a mere game with big prizes, and we have heard that in America, where the women have no vote, the loss of life in the huge steel mills is appalling; and that the number of young brakemen, fine young fellows, every one of them the pride of some mother, killed every year is beyond belief; that the average loss of life among the structural-iron workers who erect the huge office buildings and bridges is as disastrous in percentages as was the loss of life in the Battle of Bull Run. When the returns of this battle were reported to President Lincoln he burst into tears of sorrow and chagrin; but we have never heard of any President, Governor or Mayor weeping over the reports of this daily loss of life, although such reports have been presented to them by Governmental investigators; and this loss of life might easily be reduced by protective legislation."

Having thus worked themselves into a fine state of irritation, analogous to that ever-recurrent uneasiness of men in the presence of insurgent women who would interfere in the management of the State, would not these voting women add: "The trouble is that men have no imagination, or rather what they have is so prone to run in the historic direction of the glory of the battlefield, that you cannot trust them with industrial affairs. Because a crew in a battleship was once lost under circumstances which suggested perfidy the male representatives of two great Nations voted to go to war; yet in any day of the year in one of these Nations alone—the United States of America—as many men are killed through industrial accidents as this crew contained. These accidents occur under circumstances which, if not perfidious, are at least so criminally indifferent to human life as to merit Kipling's characterization that the situation is impious."

Certainly these irritated women would designate such indifference to human life as unpatriotic and unjustifiable, only to be accounted for because men have not yet learned to connect patriotism with industrial affairs.

These conscientious women responsible for the State in which life was considered of more value than wealth would furthermore say: "Then, too, you men exhibit such curious survivals of the mere savage instinct of punishment and revenge. The United States alone spends every year five hundred million dollars more on its policemen, courts and prisons than upon all its works of religion, charity and education. The price of one trial expended on a criminal early in life might save the State thousands of dollars and the man untold horrors. And yet with all this vast expenditure little is done to reduce crime. Men are kept in jails and penitentiaries where there is not even the semblance of education or reformatory measure; young men are returned over and over again to the same institution until they have grown old and gray, and in all of that time they have not once been taught a trade, nor have they been in any wise prepared to withstand the temptations of life.

"A homeless young girl looking for a lodging may be arrested for soliciting on the streets, and sent to prison for six months, although there is no proof against her save the impression of the policeman. A young girl under such suspicion may be obliged to answer the most harassing questions put to her by the city attorney, with no woman near to protect her from insult; she may be subjected to the most trying examination conducted by a physician in the presence of a policeman, and no matron to whom to appeal. At least these things happen constantly in the United States—in Chicago, for instance—but possibly not in the Scandinavian countries where juries of women sit upon such cases, women whose patience has been many times tested by wayward girls and who know the untold moral harm which may result from such a physical and psychic shock."

Then these same women would go further, and, because they had lived in a real world and had administered large affairs and were therefore not prudish and affected, would say: "Worse than anything which we have mentioned is the fact that in every man-ruled city the world over a great army of women are so set aside as outcasts that it is considered a shame to speak the mere name which designates them. Because their very existence is illegal they may be arrested whenever any police captain chooses; they may be brought before a magistrate, fined and imprisoned. The men whose money sustains their houses, supplies their tawdry clothing and provides them with intoxicating drinks and drugs, are never arrested, nor indeed are they even considered lawbreakers."

Would not these fearless women, whose concern for the morals of the family had always been able to express itself through State laws, have melted out equal punishment to men as well as to women, when they had equally transgressed the statute law?

Did the enfranchised women evoked by our imagination speak thus to the disenfranchised men, the latter would at least respect their scruples and their hesitation in regard to an extension of the obligation of citizenship. But what would be the temper of the masculine mind if the voting women representing the existing State should present to them only the following half-dozen objections, which are unhappily so familiar to many of us: If the women should say, first, that men would find politics corrupting; second, that they would doubtless vote as their wives and mothers did; third, that men's suffrage would only double the vote without changing results; fourth, that men's suffrage would diminish the respect for men; fifth, that most men do not want to vote; sixth, that the best men would not vote?

I do not believe that women broadened by life and its manifold experiences would actually present these six objections to men as real reasons for withholding the franchise from them, unless indeed they had long formed the habit of regarding men not as comrades and fellow-citizens, but as a class by themselves, in essential matters really inferior although always held sentimentally very much above them.

Certainly no such talk would be indulged in between men and women who had together embodied in political institutions the old affairs of life which had normally and historically belonged to both of them. If women had adjusted herself to the changing demands of the State as she did to the historic mutations of her own household she might naturally and without challenge have held the place in the State which she now holds in the family.

Robert K. Merton (1910–2003) stands among the most important sociologists of the twentieth century. His work has spanned across many subjects, but he is best-known for his contributions to sociological theory in the form of structural functionalism. Merton also made a significant contribution to the sociological study of crime and deviance through his refinement and expansion of Durkheim's theory of anomie. In this excerpt from his book *Social Theory and Social Structure*, Merton distinguishes between manifest (intended and conscious) functions and latent (unintended or unanticipated) functions in society. Merton then provides several rationales for the utility of the distinction.

Manifest and Latent Functions

Robert K. Merton

. . . the distinction between manifest and latent functions was devised to preclude the inadvertent confusion, often found in the sociological literature, between conscious *motivations* for social behavior and its *objective consequences*. Our scrutiny of current vocabularies of functional analysis has shown how easily, and how unfortunately, the sociologist may identify *motives* with *functions*. It was further indicated that the motive and the function vary independently and that the failure to register this fact in an established terminology has contributed to the unwitting tendency among sociologists to confuse the subjective categories of motivation with the objective categories of function. This, then, is the central purpose of our succumbing to the not-always-commendable practice of introducing new terms into the rapidly growing technical vocabulary of sociology, a practice regarded by many laymen as an affront to their intelligence and an offense against common intelligibility.

As will be readily recognized, I have adapted the terms "manifest" and "latent" from their use in another context by Freud (although Francis Bacon had long ago spoken of "latent process" and "latent configuration" in connection with processes which are below the threshold of superficial observation).

The distinction itself has been repeatedly drawn by observers of human behavior at irregular intervals over a span of many centuries.[1] Indeed, it would be disconcerting to find that a distinction which we have come to regard as central to functional analysis had not been made by any of that numerous company who have in effect adopted a functional orientation. We need mention only a few of those who have, in recent decades, found it necessary to distinguish in their specific interpretations of behavior between the end-in-view and the functional consequences of action.

---

[1] References to some of the more significant among these earlier appearances of the distinction will be found in Merton, "Unanticipated consequences of purposive action. . . ," 1936, *American Sociological Review*, 1894–1904.

George H. Mead[2]: ". . . that attitude of hostility toward the law-breaker has the unique advantage [read: latent function] of uniting all members of the community in the emotional solidarity of aggression. While the most admirable of humanitarian efforts are sure to run counter to the individual interests of very many in the community, or fail to touch the interest and imagination of the multitude and to leave the community divided or indifferent, the cry of thief or murderer is attuned to profound complexes, lying below the surface of competing individual efforts, and citizens who have [been] separated by divergent interests stand together against the common enemy."

Emile Durkheim's[3] similar analysis of the social functions of punishment is also focused on its latent functions (consequences for the community) rather than confined to manifest functions (consequences for the criminal).

W. G. Sumner[4]: ". . . from the first acts by which men try to satisfy needs, each act stands by itself, and looks no further than the immediate satisfaction. From recurrent needs arise habits for the individual and customs for the group, but these results are consequences which were never conscious, and never foreseen or intended. They are not noticed until they have long existed, and it is still longer before they are appreciated." Although this fails to locate the latent functions of standardized social actions for a designated social structure, it plainly makes the basic distinction between ends-in-view and objective consequences.

R. M. MacIver[5]: In addition to the direct effects of institutions, "there are further effects by way of control which lie outside the direct purposes of men . . . this type of reactive form of control . . . may, though unintended, be of profound service to society."

W. I. Thomas and F. Znaniecki[6]: "Although all the new [Polish peasant cooperative] institutions are thus formed with the definite purpose of satisfying certain specific needs, their social function is by no means limited to their explicit and conscious purpose . . . every one of these institutions—commune or agricultural circle, loan and savings bank, or theater—is not merely a mechanism for the management of certain values but also an association of people, each member of which is supposed to participate in the common activities as a living, concrete individual. Whatever is the predominant, official common interest upon which the institution is founded, the association as a concrete

---

[2] George H. Mead, "The psychology of punitive justice," *American Journal of Sociology*, 1918, 23, 577–602, esp. 591.

[3] As suggested earlier in this chapter, Durkheim adopted a functional orientation throughout his work, and he operates, albeit often without explicit notice, with concepts equivalent to that of latent function in all of his researches. The reference in the text at this point is to his "Deux lois de l'évolution penale," *L'année sociologique*, 1899–1900, 4, 55-95, as well as to his *Division of Labor in Society* (Glencoe, Illinois: The Free Press, 1947).

[4] This one of his many such observations is of course from W. G. Sumner's *Folkways*, (Boston: Ginn & Co., 1906), 3. His collaborator, Albert G. Keller retained the distinction in his own writings; see, for example, his *Social Evolution*, (New York: Macmillan, 1927), at 93–95.

[5] This is advisedly drawn from one of MacIver's earlier works, *Community*, (London: Macmillan, 1915). The distinction takes on greater importance in his later writings, becoming a major element in his *Social Causation*, (Boston: Ginn & Co., 1942), esp. at 314–321, and informs the greater part of his *The More Perfect Union* (New York: Macmillan, 1948).

[6] The single excerpt quoted in the text is one of scores which have led to *The Polish Peasant in Europe and America* being deservedly described as a "sociological classic." See pages 1426–7 and 1523 ff. As will be noted later in this chapter, the insights and conceptual distinctions contained in this one passage, and there are many others like it in point of richness of content, were forgotten or never noticed by those industrial sociologists who recently came to develop the notion of "informal organization" in industry.

group of human personalities unofficially involves many other interests; the social contacts between its members are not limited to their common pursuit, though the latter, of course, constitutes both the main reason for which the association is formed and the most permanent bond which holds it together. Owing to this combination of an abstract political, economic, or rather rational mechanism for the satisfaction of specific needs with the concrete unity of a social group, the new institution is also the best intermediary link between the peasant primary-group and the secondary national system."

These and numerous other sociological observers have, then, from time to time distinguished between categories of subjective disposition ("needs, interests, purposes") and categories of generally unrecognized but objective functional consequences ("unique advantages," "never conscious" consequences, "unintended . . . service to society," "function not limited to conscious and explicit purpose").

Since the occasion for making the distinction arises with great frequency, and since the purpose of a conceptual scheme is to direct observations toward salient elements of a situation and to prevent the inadvertent oversight of these elements, it would seem justifiable to designate this distinction by an appropriate set of terms. This is the rationale for the distinction between manifest functions and latent functions; the first referring to those objective consequences for a specified unit (person, subgroup, social or cultural system) which contribute to its adjustment or adaptation and were so intended; the second referring to unintended and unrecognized consequences of the same order.

There are some indications that the christening of this distinction may serve a heuristic purpose by becoming incorporated into an explicit conceptual apparatus, thus aiding both systematic observation and later analysis. In recent years, for example, the distinction between manifest and latent functions has been utilized in analyses of racial intermarriage,[7] social stratification,[8] affective frustration,[9] Veblen's sociological theories,[10] prevailing American orientations toward Russia,[11] propaganda as a means of social control,[12] Malinowski's anthropological theory,[13] Navajo witchcraft,[14] problems in the sociology of knowledge,[15] fashion,[16] the dynamics of personality,[17] national security

---

7 Merton, Robert K., "Intermarriage and the social structure," (1941), 4, 361-374.

8 Kingsley Davis, "A conceptual analysis of stratification," *American Sociological Review*, 1942, 7, 309–321.

9 Thorner, *op. cit.*, esp. at 165.

10 A. K. Davis, *Thorstein Veblen's Social Theory*, Harvard Ph.D. dissertation, 1941 and "Veblen on the decline of the Protestant Ethic," *Social Forces*, 1944, 22, 282–86; Louis Schneider, *The Freudian Psychology and Veblen's Social Theory*, New York: King's Crown Press, 1948), esp. Chapter 2.

11 A. K. Davis, "Some sources of American hostility to Russia," *American Journal of Sociology*, 1947, 53, 174–183.

12 Talcott Parsons, "Propaganda and social control," in his *Essays in Sociological Theory*.

13 Clyde Kluckhohn, "Bronislaw Malinowski, 1884–1942," *Journal of American Folklore*, 1943, 56, 208–219.

14 Clyde Kluckhohn, *Navaho Witchcraft*, *op. cit.*, esp. at 46–47 and ff.

15 Merton, Chapter XII of this volume.

16 Bernard Barber and L. S. Lobel, "Fashion in women's clothes and the American social system," *Social Forces*, 1952, 31, 124–131.

17 O. H. Mowrer and C. Kluckhohn, "Dynamic theory of personality," in J. M. Hunt, ed., *Personality and the Behavior Disorders*, (New York: Ronald Press, 1944), 1, 69–135, esp. at 72.

measures,[18] the internal social dynamics of bureaucracy,[19] and a great variety of other sociological problems.

The very diversity of these subject-matters suggests that the theoretic distinction between manifest and latent functions is not bound up with a limited and particular range of human behavior. But there still remains the large task of ferreting out the specific uses to which this distinction can be put, and it is to this large task that we devote the remaining pages of this chapter.

Heuristic Purposes of the Distinction

Clarifies the analysis of seemingly irrational social patterns

In the first place, the distinction aids the sociological interpretation of many social practices which persist even though their manifest purpose is clearly not achieved. The time-worn procedure in such instances has been for diverse, particularly lay, observers to refer to these practices as "superstitions," irrationalities," "mere inertia of tradition," *etc.* In other words, when group behavior does not—and, indeed, often cannot—attain its ostensible purpose there is an inclination to attribute its occurrence to lack of intelligence, sheer ignorance, survivals, or so-called inertia. Thus, the Hopi ceremonials designed to produce abundant rainfall may be labelled a superstitious practice of primitive folk and that is assumed to conclude the matter. It should be noted that this in no sense accounts for the group behavior. It is simply a case of name-calling; it substitutes the epithet "superstition" for an analysis of the actual role of this behavior in the life of the group. Given the concept of latent function, however, we are reminded that this behavior *may* perform a function for the group, although this function may be quite remote from the avowed purpose of the behavior.

The concept of latent function extends the observer's attention beyond the question of whether or not the behavior attains its avowed purpose. Temporarily ignoring these explicit purposes, it directs attention *toward* another range of consequences: those bearing, for example, upon the individual personalities of Hopi involved in the ceremony and upon the persistence and continuity of the larger group. Were one to confine himself to the problem of whether a manifest (purposed) function occurs, it becomes a problem, not for the sociologist, but for the meteorologist. And to be sure, our meteorologists agree that the rain ceremonial does not produce rain; but this is hardly to the point. It is merely to say that the ceremony does not have this technological use; that this purpose of the ceremony and its actual consequences do not coincide. But with the concept of latent function, we continue our inquiry, examining the consequences of the ceremony not for the rain gods or for meteorological phenomena, but for the

---

[18] Marie Jahoda and S. W. Cook, "Security measures and freedom of thought: an exploratory study of the impact of loyalty and security programs," *Yale Law Journal*, 1952, 61, 296–333.

[19] Philip Selznick, *TVA and the Grass Roots* (University of California press, 1949); A. W. Gouldner, *Patterns of Industrial Bureaucracy* (Glencoe, Illinois: The Free Press, 1954); P. M. Blau, *The Dynamics of Bureaucracy* (University of Chicago Press, 1955); A. K. Davis, "Bureaucratic patterns in Navy officer corps," *Social Forces* 1948, 27, 142–153.

groups which conduct the ceremony. And here it may be found, as many observers indicate, that the ceremonial does indeed have functions—but functions which are non-purposed or latent.

Ceremonials may fulfill the latent function of reinforcing the group identity by providing a periodic occasion on which the scattered members of a group assemble to engage in a common activity. As Durkheim among others long since indicated, such ceremonials are a means by which collective expression is afforded the sentiments which, in a further analysis, are found to be a basic source of group unity. Through the systematic application of the concept of latent function, therefore, *apparently* irrational behavior may *at times* be found to be positively functional for the group. Operating with the concept of latent function, we are not too quick to conclude that if an activity of a group does not achieve its nominal purpose, then its persistence can be described only as an instance of "inertia," "survival," or "manipulation by powerful subgroups in the society."

In point of fact, some conception like that of latent function has very often, almost invariably, been employed by social scientists observing *a standardized practice designed to achieve an objective which one knows from accredited physical science cannot be thus achieved.* This would plainly be the case, for example, with Pueblo rituals dealing with rain or fertility. *But with behavior which is not directed toward a clearly unattainable objective, sociological observers are less likely to examine the collateral or latent functions of the behavior.*

Directs attention to theoretically fruitful fields of inquiry

The distinction between manifest and latent functions serves further to direct the attention of the sociologist to precisely those realms of behavior, attitude and belief where he can most fruitfully apply his special skills. For what is his task if he confines himself to the study of manifest functions? He is then concerned very largely with determining whether a practice instituted for a particular purpose does, in fact, achieve this purpose. He will then inquire, for example, whether a new system of wage-payment achieves its avowed purpose of reducing labor turnover or of increasing output. He will ask whether a propaganda campaign has indeed gained its objective of increasing "willingness to fight" or "willingness to buy war bonds," or "tolerance toward other ethnic groups." Now, these are important, and complex, types of inquiry. But, so long as sociologists *confine* themselves to the study of manifest functions, their inquiry is set for them by practical men of affairs (whether a captain of industry, a trade union leader, or, conceivably, a Navaho chieftain, is for the moment immaterial), rather than by the theoretic problems which are at the core of the discipline. By dealing primarily with the realm of manifest functions, with the key problem of whether deliberately instituted practices or organizations succeed in achieving their objectives, the sociologist becomes converted into an industrious and skilled recorder of the altogether familiar pattern of behavior. *The terms of appraisal are fixed and limited by the question put to him by the non-theoretic men of affairs, e.g.,* has the new wage-payment program achieved such-and-such purposes?

But armed with the concept of latent function, the sociologist extends his inquiry in those very directions which promise most for the theoretic development of the discipline. He examines the familiar (or planned) social practice to ascertain the latent, and hence generally unrecognized, functions (as well, of course, as the manifest functions). He considers, for example, the consequences of the new wage plan for, say, the trade union in which the workers are organized or the consequences of a propaganda program, not only for increasing its avowed purpose of stirring up patriotic fervor, but also for making large numbers of people reluctant to speak their minds when they differ with official policies, *etc.* In short, it is suggested that the *distinctive* intellectual contributions of the sociologist are found primarily in the study of unintended consequences (among which are latent functions) of social practices, as well as in the study of anticipated consequences (among which are manifest functions).[20]

There is some evidence that it is precisely at the point where the research attention of sociologists has shifted from the plane of manifest to the plane of latent functions that they have made their *distinctive* and major contributions. This can be extensively documented but a few passing illustrations must suffice.

The Hawthorne Western Electric Studies[21]

As is well known, the early stages of this inquiry were concerned with the problem of the relations of "illumination to efficiency" of industrial workers. For some two and a half years, attention was focused on problems such as this: do variations in the intensity of lighting affect production? The initial results showed that within wide limits there was no uniform relation between illumination and output. Production output increased *both* in the experimental group where illumination was increased (or *decreased*) *and* in the control group where no changes in illumination were introduced. In short, the investigators confined themselves wholly to a search for the manifest functions. Lacking a concept of latent social function, no attention whatever was initially paid to the social consequences *of the experiment* for relations among members of the test and control groups or for relations between workers and the test room authorities. In other words, the investigators lacked a sociological frame of reference and operated merely as "engineers" (just as a group of meteorologists might have explored the "effects" upon rainfall of the Hopi ceremonial).

Only after continued investigation, did it occur to the research group to explore the consequences of the new "experimental situation" for the self-images and self-conceptions of the workers taking part in the experiment, for the interpersonal relations among members of the group, for the coherence and

[20] For a brief illustration of this general proposition, see Robert K. Merton, Marjorie Fiske and Alberta Curtis, *Mass Persuasion*, (New York: Harper, 1946), 185–189; Jahoda and Cook, *op. cit.*

[21] This is cited as a case study of how *an elaborate research was wholly changed in theoretic orientation and in the character of its research findings by the introduction of a concept approximating the concept of latent function.* Selection of the case for this purpose does not, of course, imply full acceptance of the *interpretations* which the authors give their findings. Among the several volumes reporting the Western Electric research, see particularly F. J. Roethlisberger and W. J. Dickson, *Management and the Worker*, (Harvard University Press, 1939).

unity of the group. As Elton Mayo reports it, "the illumination fiasco had made them alert to the need that very careful records should be kept of everything that happened in the room in addition to the obvious engineering and industrial devices. Their observations therefore included not only records of industrial and engineering changes but also records of physiological or medical changes, and, *in a sense*, of social and anthropological. This last took the form of a 'log' that gave as full an account as possible of the actual events of every day. . . ."[22] In short, it was only after a long series of experiments which wholly neglected the latent social functions of the experiment (as a contrived social situation) that this distinctly sociological framework was introduced. "With this realization," the authors write, "the inquiry changed its character. No longer were the investigators interested in testing for the effects of single variables. In the place of a controlled experiment, they substituted the notion of a social situation which needed to be described and understood as a system of interdependent elements." Thereafter, as is now widely known, inquiry was directed very largely toward ferreting out the latent functions of standardized practices among the workers, of informal organization developing among workers, of workers' games instituted by "wise administrators," of large programs of worker counselling and interviewing, *etc.* The new conceptual scheme entirely altered the range and types of data gathered in the ensuing research.

One has only to return to the previously quoted excerpt from Thomas and Znaniecki in their classical work of some thirty years ago, to recognize the correctness of Shils' remark:

> . . . indeed the history of the study of primary groups in American sociology is a supreme instance of the *discontinuities of the development of this discipline*: a problem is stressed by one who is an acknowledged founder of the discipline, the problem is left unstudied, then, some years later, it is taken up with enthusiasm as if no one had ever thought of it before.[23]

For Thomas and Znaniecki had repeatedly emphasized the sociological view that, whatever its major purpose, "the association as a concrete group of human personalities unofficially involves many other interests; the social contacts between its members are not limited to their common pursuit . . ." In effect, then, it had taken years of experimentation to turn the attention of the Western Electric research team to the latent social functions of primary groups emerging in industrial organizations. It should be made clear that this case is not cited here as an instance of defective experimental design; that is not our immediate concern. It is considered only as an illustration of the pertinence for *sociological* inquiry of the concept of latent function, and the associated concepts of functional analysis. It illustrates how the inclusion of this concept (whether the term is used or not is inconsequential) can sensitize sociological investigators to a range of significant social variables which are otherwise easily overlooked. The

[22] Elton Mayo, *The Social Problems of an Industrial Civilization*, (Harvard University Press, 1945), 70.

[23] Edward Shils, *The Present State of American Sociology*, (Glencoe, Illinois. The Free Press, 1948), 42 [italics supplied].

explicit ticketing of the concept may perhaps lessen the frequency of such occasions of discontinuity in future sociological research.

The discovery of latent functions represents significant increments in sociological knowledge

There is another respect in which inquiry into latent functions represents a distinctive contribution of the social scientist. It is precisely the latent functions of a practice or belief which are not common knowledge, for these are unintended and generally unrecognized social and psychological consequences. As a result, findings concerning latent functions represent a greater increment in knowledge than findings concerning manifest functions. They represent, also, greater departures from "common-sense" knowledge about social life. Inasmuch as the latent functions depart, more or less, from the avowed manifest functions, the research which uncovers latent functions very often produces "paradoxical" results. The seeming paradox arises from the sharp modification of a familiar popular preconception which regards a standardized practice or belief *only* in terms of its manifest functions by indicating some of its subsidiary or collateral latent functions. The introduction of the concept of latent function in social research leads to conclusions which show that "social life is not as simple as it first seems." For as long as people confine themselves to *certain* consequences (*e.g.* manifest consequences), it is comparatively simple for them to pass moral judgments upon the practice or belief in question. Moral evaluations, generally based on these manifest consequences, tend to be polarized in terms of black or white. But the perception of further (latent) consequences often complicates the picture. Problems of moral evaluation (which are not our immediate concern) and problems of social engineering (which are our concern[24]) both take on the additional complexities usually involved in responsible social decisions.

An example of inquiry which implicitly uses the notion of latent function will illustrate the sense in which "paradox"—discrepancy between the apparent, merely manifest, function and the actual, which also includes latent functions—tends to occur as a result of including this concept. Thus, to revert to Veblen's well-known analysis of conspicuous consumption, it is no accident that he has been recognized as a social analyst gifted with an eye for the paradoxical, the ironic, the satiric. For these are frequent, if not inevitable, outcomes of applying the concept of latent function (or its equivalent).

The Pattern of Conspicuous Consumption

The manifest purpose of buying consumption goods is, of course, the satisfaction of the needs for which these goods are explicitly designed. Thus, auto-

[24]This is not to deny that social engineering has direct moral implications or that technique and morality are inescapably intertwined, but I do not intend to deal with this range of problems in the present chapter. For some discussion of these problems see chapters VI, XV and XVII; also Merton, Fiske and Curtis, *Mass Persuasion*, chapter 7.

mobiles are obviously intended to provide a certain kind of transportation; candles, to provide light; choice articles of food to provide sustenance; rare art products to provide aesthetic pleasure. Since these products *do* have these uses, it was largely assumed that these encompass the range of socially significant functions. Veblen indeed suggests that this was ordinarily the prevailing view (in the pre-Veblenian era, of course): "The end of acquisition and accumulation is conventionally held to be the consumption of the goods accumulated. . . . This is at least felt to be the economically legitimate end of acquisition, *which alone it is incumbent on the theory to take account of.*"[25]

However, says Veblen in effect, as sociologists we must go on to consider the latent functions of acquisition, accumulation and consumption, and these latent functions are remote indeed from the manifest functions. "But, it is only when taken in a sense far removed from its naive meaning [*i.e.* manifest function] that the consumption of goods can be said to afford the incentive from which accumulation invariably proceeds." And among these latent functions, which help explain the persistence and the social location of the pattern of conspicuous consumption, is its symbolization of "pecuniary strength and so of gaining or retaining a good name." The exercise of "punctilious discrimination" in the excellence of "food, drink, shelter, service, ornaments, apparel, amusements" results not merely in direct gratifications derived from the consumption of "superior" to "inferior" articles, but also, and Veblen argues, more importantly, it results in a *heightening or reaffirmation of social status.*

The Veblenian paradox is that people buy expensive goods not so much because they are superior but because they are expensive. For it is the latent equation ("costliness = mark of higher social status") which he singles out in his functional analysis, rather than the manifest equation ("costliness = excellence of the goods"). Not that he denies manifest functions *any* place in buttressing the pattern of conspicuous consumption. These, too, are operative. "What has just been said must not be taken to mean that there are no other incentives to acquisition and accumulation than this desire to excel in pecuniary standing and so gain the esteem and envy of one's fellowmen. The desire for added comfort and security from want is present as a motive at every stage. . . ." Or again: "It would be hazardous to assert that a useful purpose is ever absent from the utility of any article or of any service, however obviously its prime purpose and chief element is conspicuous waste" and derived social esteem.[26] It is only that *these direct, manifest functions do not fully account for the prevailing patterns of consumption. Otherwise put, if the latent functions of status-enhancement or status-reaffirmation*

[25] Veblen, Thorstein. *Theory of Leisure Class,* (Vanguard Press, New York) 1928.

[26] *Ibid.*, 32, 101. It will be noted throughout that Veblen is given to loose terminology. In the marked passages (and repeatedly elsewhere) he uses "incentive," "desire," "purpose," and "function" interchangeably. Since the context usually makes clear the denotation of these terms, no great harm is done. But it is clear that the expressed purposes of conformity to a culture pattern are by no means identical with the latent functions of the conformity. Veblen occasionally recognizes this. For example, "In strict accuracy nothing should be included under the head of conspicuous waste but such expenditure as is incurred on the ground of an invidious pecuniary comparison. But in order to bring any given item or element in under this head *it is not necessary that it should be recognized as waste in this sense by the person incurring the expenditure.*" (Ibid. 99; italics supplied). Cf. A. K. Davis, "Veblen on the decline of the Protestant Ethic," *op. cit.*

were removed from the patterns of conspicuous consumption, these patterns would undergo severe changes of a sort which the "conventional" economist could not foresee.

In these respects, Veblen's analysis of latent functions departs from the common-sense notion that the end-product of consumption is "of course, the direct satisfaction which it provides": "People eat caviar because they're hungry; buy Cadillacs because they want the best car they can get; have dinner by candlelight because they like the peaceful atmosphere." The common-sense interpretation in terms of selected manifest motives gives way, in Veblen's analysis, to the collateral latent functions which are also, and perhaps more significantly, fulfilled by these practices. To be sure, the Veblenian analysis has, in the last decades, entered so fully into popular thought, that these latent functions are now widely recognized. [This raises the interesting problem of the changes occurring in a prevailing pattern of behavior when its *latent* functions become generally recognized (and are thus no longer latent). There will be no occasion for discussing this important problem in the present publication.]

The discovery of latent functions does not merely render conceptions of the functions served by certain social patterns more precise (as is the case also with studies of manifest functions), but introduces a *qualitatively different increment in the previous state of knowledge.*

Precludes the substitution of naive moral judgments for sociological analysis

Since moral evaluations in a society tend to be largely in terms of the manifest consequences of a practice or code, we should be prepared to find that analysis in terms of latent functions at times runs counter to prevailing moral evaluations. For it does not follow that the latent functions will operate in the same fashion as the manifest consequences which are ordinarily the basis of these judgments. Thus, in large sectors of the American population, the political machine or the "political racket" are judged as unequivocally "bad" and "undesirable." The grounds for such moral judgment vary somewhat, but they consist substantially in pointing out that political machines violate moral codes: political patronage violates the code of selecting personnel on the basis of impersonal qualifications rather than on grounds of party loyalty or contributions to the party war-chest; bossism violates the code that votes should be based on individual appraisal of the qualifications of candidates and of political issues, and not on abiding loyalty to a feudal leader; bribery, and "honest graft" obviously offend the proprieties of property; "protection" for crime clearly violates the law and the mores; and so on.

In view of the manifold respects in which political machines, in varying degrees, run counter to the mores and at times to the law, it becomes pertinent to inquire how they manage to continue in operation. The familiar "explanations" for the continuance of the political machine are not here in point. To be sure, it may well be that if "respectable citizenry" would live up to their political obligations, if the electorate were to be alert and enlightened; if the number of elective officers were substantially reduced from the dozens, even hundreds, which the average voter is now expected to appraise in the course of town, county, state and national elections; if the electorate were activated by the "wealthy and educated classes without whose participation," as the not-always democratically oriented Bryce put it, "the best-framed government must speedily degenerate";—if these and a plethora of similar changes in political structure were introduced, perhaps the "evils" of the political machine would indeed be exorcized.[27] But it should be noted that these changes are often not introduced, that political machines have had the phoenix-like quality of arising strong and unspoiled from their ashes, that, in short, this structure has exhibited a notable vitality in many areas of American political life.

Proceeding from the functional view, therefore, that we should *ordinarily* (not invariably) expect persistent social patterns and social structures to perform positive functions *which are at the time not adequately fulfilled by other existing patterns and structures*, the thought occurs that perhaps this publicly maligned organization is, *under present conditions*, satisfying basic latent functions.[28] A brief examination of current analyses of this type of structure may also serve to illustrate additional problems of functional analysis.

[27] These "explanations" are "causal" in design. They profess to indicate the social conditions under which political machines come into being. In so far as they are empirically confirmed, these explanations of course add to our knowledge concerning the problem: how is it that political machines operate in certain areas and not in others? How do they manage to continue? *But these causal accounts are not sufficient*. The functional consequences of the machine, as we shall see, go far toward supplementing the causal interpretation.

[28] I trust it is superfluous to add that this hypothesis is not "in support of the political machine." The question whether the dysfunctions of the machine outweigh its functions, the question whether alternative structures are not available which may fulfill its functions without necessarily entailing its social dysfunctions, still remain to be considered at an appropriate point. We are here concerned with documenting the statement that moral judgments based *entirely* on an appraisal of manifest functions of a social structure are "unrealistic" in the strict sense, *i.e.*, they do not take into account other actual consequences of that structure, consequences which may provide basic social support for the structure. As will be indicated later, "social reforms" or "social engineering" which ignore latent functions do so on pain of suffering acute disappointments and boomerang effects.

George Herbert Mead's (1863–1931) posthumously published lectures that form the substance of the book *Mind, Self, and Society* represent important statements on the relationship between individual and society. Mead maintained that the self arises in social interaction with others through symbolic communication. His work became the basis for the school of thought in sociology known as symbolic interactionism. In this selection Mead explains the emergence of self by exploring "game and play" activities of children, as well as how people come to infer the perspective of others and the larger society in which they live.

SELF AND SOCIETY

George Herbert Mead

The self, as that which can be an object to itself, is essentially a social structure, and it arises in social experience. After a self has arisen, it in a certain sense provides for itself its social experiences, and so we can conceive of an absolutely solitary self. But it is impossible to conceive of a self arising outside of social experience. When it has arisen we can think of a person in solitary confinement for the rest of his life, but who still has himself as a companion, and is able to think and to converse with himself as he had communicated with others. That process to which I have just referred, of responding to one's self as another responds to it, taking part in one's own conversation with others, being aware of what one is saying and using that awareness of what one is saying to determine what one is going to say there-after—that is a process with which we are all familiar. We are continually following up our own address to other persons by an understanding of what we are saying, and using that understanding in the direction of our continued speech. We are finding out what we are going to say, what we are going to do, by saying and doing, and in the process we are continually controlling the process itself. In the conversation of gestures what we say calls out a certain response in another and that in turn changes our own action, so that we shift from what we started to do because of the reply the other makes. The conversation of gestures is the beginning of communication. The individual comes to carry on a conversation of gestures with himself. He says something, and that calls out a certain reply in himself which makes him change what he was going to say. One starts to say something, we will presume an unpleasant something, but when he starts to say it he realizes it is cruel. The effect on himself of what he is saying checks him; there is here a conversation of gestures between the individual and himself. We mean by significant speech that the action is one that affects the individual himself, and that the effect upon the individual himself is part of the intelligent carrying-out of the conversation with others. Now we, so to speak, amputate that social phase and dispense with it for the time being, so that one is talking to one's self as one would talk to another person.

This process of abstraction cannot be carried on indefinitely. One inevitably seeks an audience, has to pour himself out to somebody. In reflective intelligence one thinks to act, and to act solely so that this action remains a part of a social process. Thinking becomes preparatory to social action. The very process of thinking is, of course, simply an inner conversation that goes on, but it is a conversation of gestures which in its completion implies the expression of that which one thinks to an audience. One separates the significance of what he is saying to others from the actual speech and gets it ready before saying it. He thinks it out, and perhaps writes it in the form of a book; but it is still a part of social intercourse in which one is addressing other persons and at the same time addressing one's self, and in which one controls the address to other persons by the response made to one's own gesture. That the person should be responding to himself is necessary to the self, and it is this sort of social conduct which provides behavior within which that self appears. I know of no other form of behavior than the linguistic in which the individual is an object to himself, and, so far as I can see, the individual is not a self in the reflexive sense unless he is an object to himself. It is this fact that gives a critical importance to communication, since this is a type of behavior in which the individual does so respond to himself.

We realize in everyday conduct and experience that an individual does not mean a great deal of what he is doing and saying. We frequently say that such an individual is not himself. We come away from an interview with a realization that we have left out important things, that there are parts of the self that did not get into what was said. What determines the amount of the self that gets into communication is the social experience itself. Of course, a good deal of the self does not need to get expression. We carry on a whole series of different relationships to different people. We are one thing to one man and another thing to another. There are parts of the self which exist only for the self in relationship to itself. We divide ourselves up in all sorts of different selves with reference to our acquaintances. We discuss politics with one and religion with another. There are all sorts of different selves answering to all sorts of different social reactions. It is the social process itself that is responsible for the appearance of the self; it is not there as a self apart from this type of experience. . . .

. . . The unity and structure of the (complete self) reflects the unity and structure of the social process as a whole; and each of the elementary selves of which it is composed reflects the unity and structure of one of the various aspects of that process in which the individual is implicated. In other words, the various elementary selves which constitute, or are organized into, a complete self are the various aspects of the structure of that complete self answering to the various aspects of the structure of the social process as a whole; the structure of the complete self is thus a reflection of the complete social process. The organization and unification of a social group is identical with the organization and unification of any one of the selves arising within the social process in which that group is engaged, or which it is carrying on.

The phenomenon of dissociation of personality is caused by a breaking up of the complete, unitary self into the component selves of which it is composed, and which respectively correspond to different aspects of the social process in which the person is involved, and within which his complete or unitary self has arisen; these aspects being the different social groups to which he belongs within that process. . . .

. . . The peculiar character possessed by our human social environment belongs to it by virtue of the peculiar character of human social activity; and that character, as we have seen, is to be found in the process of communication, and more particularly in the triadic relation on which the existence of meaning is based: the relation of the gesture of one organism to the adjustive response made to it by another organism, in its indicative capacity as pointing to the completion or resultant of the act it initiates (the meaning of the gesture being thus the response of the second organism to it as such, or as a gesture). What, as it were, takes the gesture out of the social act and isolates it as such—what makes it something more than just an early phase of an individual act—is the response of another organism, or of other organisms, to it. Such a response is its meaning, or gives it its meaning. The social situation and process of behavior are here presupposed by the acts of the individual organisms implicated therein. The gesture arises as a separable element . . .

. . . Our symbols are all universal. You cannot say anything that is absolutely particular; anything you say that has any meaning at all is universal. You are saying something that calls out a specific response in anybody else provided that the symbol exists for him in his experience as it does for you. There is the language of speech and the language of hands, and there may be the language of the expression of the countenance. One can register grief or joy and call out certain responses. There are primitive people who can carry on elaborate conversations just by expressions of the countenance. Even in these cases the person who communicates is affected by that expression just as he expects somebody else to be affected. Thinking always implies a symbol which will call out the same response in another that it calls out in the thinker. Such a symbol is a universal of discourse; it is universal in its character. We always assume that the symbol we use is one which will call out in the other person the same response, provided it is a part of his mechanism of conduct. A person who is saying something is saying to himself what he says to others; otherwise he does not know what he is talking about. . . .

. . . What is essential to communication is that the symbol should arouse in one's self what it arouses in the other individual. It must have that sort of universality to any person who finds himself in the same situation. There is a possibility of language whenever a stimulus can affect the individual as it affects the other. With a blind person such as Helen Keller, it is a contact experience that could be given to another as it is given to herself. It is out of that sort of language that the mind of Helen Keller was built up. As she has recognized, it was not until she could get into communication with other persons through symbols which could arouse in herself the responses they arouse in other people that she could get what we term a mental content, or a self.

Another set of background factors in the genesis of the self is represented in the activities of play and the game.

Among primitive people, as I have said, the necessity of distinguishing the self and the organism was recognized in what we term the "double": the individual has a thing-like self that is affected by the individual as it affects other people and which is distinguished from the immediate organism in that it can leave the body and come back to it. This is the basis for the concept of the soul as a separate entity.

We find in children something that answers to this double, namely, the invisible, imaginary companions which a good many children produce in their own experience. They organize in this way the responses which they call out in other persons and call out also in themselves. Of course, this playing with an imaginary companion is only a peculiarly interesting phase of ordinary play. Play in this sense, especially the stage which precedes the organized games, is a play at something. A child plays at being a mother, at being a teacher, at being a policeman; that is, it is taking different roles, as we say. . . .

. . . If we contrast play with the situation in an organized game, we note the essential difference that the child who plays in a game must be ready to take the attitude of everyone else involved in that game, and that these different roles must have a definite relationship to each other. Taking a very simple game such as hide-and-seek, everyone with the exception of the one who is hiding is a person who is hunting. A child does not require more than the person who is hunted and the one who is hunting. If a child is playing in the first sense he just goes on playing, but there is no basic organization gained. In that early stage he passes from one role to another just as a whim takes him. But in a game where a number of individuals are involved, then the child taking one role must be ready to take the role of everyone else. If he gets in a ball nine he must have the responses of each position involved in his own position. He must know what everyone else is going to do in order to carry out his own play. He has to take all of these roles. They do not all have to be present in consciousness at the same time, but at some moments he has to have three or four individuals present in his own attitude, such as the one who is going to throw the ball, the one who is going to catch it, and so on. These responses must be, in some degree, present in his own make-up. In the game, then, there is a set of responses of such others so organized that the attitude of one calls out the appropriate attitudes of the other.

This organization is put in the form of the rules of the game. Children take a great interest in rules. They make rules on the spot in order to help themselves out of difficulties. Part of the enjoyment of the game is to get these rules. Now, the rules are the set of responses which a particular attitude calls out. You can demand a certain response in others if you take a certain attitude. These responses are all in yourself as well. There you get an organized set of such responses as that to which I have referred, which is something more elaborate than the roles found in play. Here there is just a set of responses that follow on each other indefinitely. At such a stage we speak of a child as not yet having a fully developed self. The child responds in a fairly intelligent fashion to the immediate stimuli that come to him, but they are not organized. He does not organize his life as we would like to have him do, namely, as a whole. There is just a set of responses of the type of play. The child reacts to a certain stimulus, and the reaction is in himself that is called out in others, but he is not a whole self. In his game he has to have an organization of these roles; otherwise he cannot play the game. The game represents the passage in the life of the child from taking the role of others in play to the organized part that is essential to self-consciousness in the full sense of the term. . . .

. . . The fundamental difference between the game and play is that in the latter the child must have the attitude of all the others involved in that game. The attitudes of the other players which the participant assumes organize into a sort of unit, and it is that organization which controls the response of the individual. The illustration used was of a person playing baseball. Each one of his own acts is determined by his assumption of the action of the others who are playing the game. What he does is controlled by his being everyone else on that team, at least in so far as those attitudes affect his own particular response. We get then an "other" which is an organization of the attitudes of those involved in the same process.

The organized community or social group which gives to the individual his unity of self may be called "the generalized other." The attitude of the generalized other is the attitude of the whole community. Thus, for example, in the case of such a social group as a ball team, the team is the generalized other in so far as it enters—as an organized process or social activity—into the experience of any one of the individual members of it.

If the given human individual is to develop a self in the fullest sense, it is not sufficient for him merely to take the attitudes of other human individuals toward himself and toward one another within the human social process, and to bring that social process as a whole into his individual experience merely in these terms: he must also, in the same way that he takes the attitudes of other individuals toward himself and toward one another, take their attitudes toward the various phases or aspects of the common social activity or set of social undertakings in which, as members of an organized society or social group, they are all engaged; and he must then, by generalizing these individual attitudes of that organized society or social group itself, as a whole, act toward different social projects which at any given time it is carrying out, or toward the various larger phases of the general social process which constitutes its life and of which these projects are specific manifestations. This getting of the broad activities of any given social whole or organized society as such within the experiential field of any one of the individuals involved or included in that whole is, in other words, the essential basis and prerequisite of the fullest development of that individual's self: only in so far as he takes the attitudes of the organized social group to which he belongs toward the organized, co-operative social activity or set of such activities in which that group as such is engaged, does he develop a complete self or possess the sort of complete self he has developed. And on the other hand, the complex co-operative processes and activities and institutional functionings of organized human society are also possible only in so far as every individual involved in them or belonging to that society can take the general attitudes of all other such individuals with reference to these processes and activities and institutional functionings, and to the organized social whole of experiential relations and interactions thereby constituted—and can direct his own behavior accordingly.

It is in the form of the generalized other that the social process influences the behavior of the individuals involved in it and carrying it on, i.e., that the community exercises control over the conduct of its individual members; for it is in this form that the social process or community enters as a determining factor into the individual's thinking. In abstract thought the individual takes the attitude of the generalized other toward himself, without reference to its expression in any particular other individuals; and in concrete thought he takes that attitude in so far as it is expressed in the attitudes toward his behavior of those other individuals with whom he is involved in the given social situation or act. But only by taking the attitude of the generalized other toward himself, in one or another of these ways, can he think at all; for only thus can thinking—or the internalized conversation of gestures which constitutes thinking—occur. And only through the taking by individuals of the attitude or attitudes of the generalized other toward themselves is the existence of a universe of discourse, as that system of common or social meanings which thinking presupposes at its context, rendered possible.

The self-conscious human individual, then, takes or assumes the organized social attitudes of the given social group or community (or of some one section thereof) to which he belongs, toward the social problems of various kinds which confront that group or community at any given time, and which arise in connection with the correspondingly different social projects or organized co-operative enterprises in which that group or community as such is engaged; and as an individual participant in these social projects or co-operative enterprises, he governs his own conduct accordingly. In politics, for example, the individual identifies himself with an entire political party and takes the organized attitudes of that entire party toward the rest of the given social community and toward the problems which confront the party within the given social situation; and he consequently reacts or responds in terms of the organized attitudes of the party as a whole. He thus enters into a special set of social relations with all the other individuals who belong to that political party; and in the same way he enters into various other special sets of social relations, with various other classes of individuals respectively, the individuals of each of these classes being the other members of some one of the particular organized subgroups (determined in socially functional terms) of which he himself is a member within the entire given society or social community. In the most highly developed, organized, and complicated human social communities—those evolved by civilized man—these various socially functional classes or subgroups of individuals to which any given individual belongs (and with the other individual members of which he thus enters into a special set of social relations) are of two kinds. Some of them are concrete social classes or subgroups, such as political parties, clubs, corporations, which are all actually functional social units, in terms of which their individual members are directly related to one another. The others are abstract social classes or subgroups, such as the class of debtors and the class of creditors, in terms of which their individual members are related to one another only more or less indirectly, and which only more or less indirectly function as social units, but which afford or represent unlimited possibilities for the widening and ramifying and enriching of the social relations among all the individual members of the given society as an organized and unified whole. The given individual's membership in several of these abstract social classes or subgroups makes possible his entrance into definite social relations (however indirect) with an almost infinite number of other individuals who also belong to or are included within one or another of these abstract social classes or subgroups cutting across functional lines of demarcation which divide different human social communities from one another, and including individual members from several (in some cases from all) such communities. Of these abstract social classes or subgroups of human individuals the one which is most inclusive and extensive is, of course, the one defined by the logical universe of discourse (or system of universally significant symbols) determined by the participation and communicative interaction of individuals; for of all such classes or subgroups, it is the one which claims the largest number of individual members, and which enables the largest conceivable number of human individuals to enter into some sort of social relation, however indirect or abstract it may be, with one another—a relation arising from the universal functioning of gestures as significant symbols in the general human social process of communication.

I have pointed out, then, that there are two general stages in the full development of the self. At the first of these stages, the individual's self is constituted simply by an organization of the particular attitudes of other individuals toward himself and toward one another in the specific social acts in which he participates with them. But at the second stage in the full development of the individual's self that self is constituted not only by an organization of these particular individual attitudes, but also by an organization of the social attitudes of the generalized other or the social group as a whole to which he belongs. These social or group attitudes are brought within the individual's field of direct experience, and are included as elements in the structure or constitution of his self, in the same way that the attitudes of particular other individuals are; and the individual arrives at them, or succeeds in taking them, by means of further organizing, and then generalizing, the attitudes of particular other individuals in terms of their organized social bearings and implications. So the self reaches its full development by organizing these individual attitudes of others into the organized social or group attitudes, and by thus becoming an individual reflection of the general systematic pattern of social or group behavior in which it and the others are all involved—a pattern which enters as a whole into the individual's experience in terms of these organized group attitudes which, through the mechanism of his central nervous system, he takes toward himself, just as he takes the individual attitudes of others.

The game has a logic, so that such an organization of the self is rendered possible: there is a definite end to be obtained; the actions of the different individuals are all related to each other with reference to that end so that they do not conflict; one is not in conflict with himself in the attitude of another man on the team. If one has the attitude of the person throwing the ball he can also have the response of catching the ball. The two are related so that they further the purpose of the game itself. They are interrelated in a unitary, organic fashion. There is a definite unity, then, which is introduced into the organization of other selves when we reach such a stage as that of the game, as over against the situation of play where there is a simple succession of one role after another, a situation which is, of course, characteristic of the child's own personality. The child is one thing at one time and another at another, and what he is at one moment does not determine what he is at another. That is both the charm of childhood as well as its inadequacy. You cannot count on the child; you cannot assume that all the things he does are going to determine what he will do at any moment. He is not organized into a whole. The child has no definite character, no definite personality.

The game is then an illustration of the situation out of which an organized personality arises. In so far as the child does take the attitude of the other and allows that attitude of the other to determine the thing he is going to do with reference to a common end, he is becoming an organic member of society. He is taking over the morale of that society and is becoming an essential member of it. He belongs to it in so far as he does allow the attitude of the other that he takes to control his own immediate expression. What is involved here is some sort of an organized process. That which is expressed in terms of the game is, of course, being continually expressed in the social life of the child, but this wider process goes beyond the immediate experience of the child himself. The importance of the game is that it lies entirely inside of the child's own experience, and the importance of our modern type of education is that it is brought as far as possible within this realm. The different attitudes that a child assumes are so organized that they exercise a definite control over his response, as the attitudes in a game control his own immediate response. In the game we get an organized other, a generalized other, which is found in the nature of the child itself, and finds its expression in the immediate experience of the child. And it is that organized activity in the child's own nature controlling the particular response which gives unity, and which builds up his own self.

What goes on in the game goes on in the life of the child all the time. He is continually taking the attitudes of those about him, especially the roles of those who in some sense control him and on whom he depends. He gets the function of the process in an abstract sort of a way at first. It goes over from the play into the game in a real sense. He has to play the game. The morale of the game takes hold of the child more than the larger morale of the whole community. The child passes into the game and the game expresses a social situation in which he can completely enter; its morale may have a greater hold on him than that of the family to which he belongs or the community in which he lives. There are all sorts of social organizations, some of which are fairly lasting, some temporary, into which the child is entering, and he is playing a sort of social game in them. It is a period in which he likes "to belong," and he gets into organizations which come into existence and pass out of existence. He becomes a something which can function in the organized whole, and thus tends to determine himself in his relationship with the group to which he belongs. That process is one which is a striking stage in the development of the child's morale. It constitutes him a self-conscious member of the community to which he belongs.

Such is the process by which a personality arises. I have spoken of this as a process in which a child takes the role of the other, and said that it takes place essentially through the use of language. Language is predominantly based on the vocal gesture by means of which co-operative activities in a community are carried out. Language in its significant sense is that vocal gesture which tends to arouse in the individual the attitude which it arouses in others, and it is this perfecting of the self by the gesture which mediates the social activities that gives rise to the process of taking the role of the other. The latter phrase is a little unfortunate because it suggests an actor's attitude which is actually more sophisticated than that which is involved in our own experience. To this degree it does not correctly describe that which I have in mind. We see the process most definitely in a primitive form in those situations where the child's play takes different roles. Here the very fact that he is ready to pay out money, for instance, arouses the attitude of the person who receives money; the very process is calling out in him the corresponding activities of the other person involved. The individual stimulates himself to the response which he is calling out in the other person, and then acts in some degree in response to that situation. In play the child does definitely act out the role which he himself has aroused in himself. It is that which gives, as I have said, a definite content in the individual which answers to the stimulus that affects him as it affects somebody else. The content of the other that enters into one personality is the response in the individual which his gesture calls out in the other. . . .

. . . I have so far emphasized what I have called the structures upon which the self is constructed, the framework of the self, as it were. Of course we are not only what is common to all: each one of the selves is different from everyone else; but there has to be such a common structure as I have sketched in order that we may be members of a community at all. We cannot be ourselves unless we are also members in whom there is a community of attitudes which control the attitudes of all. We cannot have rights unless we have common attitudes. That which we have acquired as self-conscious persons makes us such members of society and gives us selves. Selves can only exist in definite relationships to other selves. No hard-and-fast line can be drawn between our own selves and the selves of others, since our own selves exist and enter as such into our experience only in so far as the selves of others exist and enter as such into our experience also. The individual possesses a self only in relation to the selves of the other members of his social group; and the structure of his self expresses or reflects the general behavior pattern of this social group to which he belongs, just as does the structure of the self of every other individual belonging to this social group. . . .

. . . The self is not so much a substance as a process in which the conversation of gestures has been internalized within an organic form. This process does not exist for itself, but is simply a phase of the whole social organization of which the individual is a part. The organization of the social act has been imported into the organism and becomes then the mind of the individual. It still includes the attitudes of others, but now highly organized, so that they become what we call social attitudes rather than roles of separate individuals. This process of relating one's own organism to the others in the interactions that are going on, in so far as it is imported into the conduct of the individual with the conversation of the "I" and the "me," constitutes the self. . . .

. . . The "I" is the response of the organism to the attitudes of the others; the "me" is the organized set of attitudes of others which one himself assumes. The attitudes of the others constitute the organized "me," and then one reacts toward that as an "I."

Erving Goffman (1922–1982) developed a dramaturgical theory of the self and society inspired by Mead's basic conception of social interaction. In the selection below, excerpted from the book *The Presentation of Self in Everyday Life*, Goffman presents a theory that likens social interaction to the theater. Individuals can be seen as performers, audience members, and outsiders that operate within particular "stages" or social spaces. Goffman suggests that how we present our selves to others is aimed toward "impression management," which is a conscious decision on the part of the individual to reveal certain aspects of the self and to conceal others, as actors do when performing on stage.

The Presentation of Self in Everyday Life

Erving Goffman

The Framework

A social establishment is any place surrounded by fixed barriers to perception in which a particular kind of activity regularly takes place. I have suggested that any social establishment may be studied profitably from the point of view of impression management. Within the walls of a social establishment we find a team of performers who cooperate to present to an audience a given definition of the situation. This will include the conception of own team and of audience and assumptions concerning the ethos that is to be maintained by rules of politeness and decorum. We often find a division into back region, where the performance of a routine is prepared, and front region, where the performance is presented. Access to these regions is controlled in order to prevent the audience from seeing backstage and to prevent outsiders from coming into a performance that is not addressed to them. Among members of the team we find that familiarity prevails, solidarity is likely to develop, and that secrets that could give the show away are shared and kept. A tacit agreement is maintained between performers and audience to act as if a given degree of opposition and of accord existed between them. Typically, but not always, agreement is stressed and opposition is underplayed. The resulting working consensus tends to be contradicted by the attitude toward the audience which the performers express in the absence of the audience and by carefully controlled communication out of character conveyed by the performers while the audience is present. We find that discrepant roles develop: some of the individuals who are apparently teammates, or audience, or outsiders acquire information about the performance and relations to the team which are not apparent and which complicate the problem of putting on a show. Sometimes disruptions occur through unmeant gestures, faux pas, and scenes, thus discrediting or contradicting the definition of the situation that is being maintained. The mythology of the team will dwell upon these disruptive events. We find that performers, audience, and outsiders all utilize techniques for saving the show, whether by avoiding likely disruptions or by correcting for unavoided ones, or by making it possible for others to do so. To ensure that these techniques will be employed, the team will tend to select members who are loyal, disciplined, and circumspect, and to select an audience that is tactful.

These features and elements, then, comprise the framework I claim to be characteristic of much social interaction as it occurs in natural settings in our Anglo-American society. This framework is formal and abstract in the sense that it can be applied to any social establishment; it is not, however, merely a static classification. The framework bears upon dynamic issues created by the motivation to sustain a definition of the situation that has been projected before others.

The Analytical Context

This report has been chiefly concerned with social establishments as relatively closed systems. It has been assumed that the relation of one establishment to others is itself an intelligible area of study and ought to be treated analytically as part of a different order of fact—the order of institutional integration. It might be well here to try to place the perspective taken in this report in the context of other perspectives which seem to be the ones currently employed, implicitly or explicitly, in the study of social establishments as closed systems. Four such perspectives may be tentatively suggested.

An establishment may be viewed "technically," in terms of its efficiency and inefficiency as an intentionally organized system of activity for the achievement of predefined objectives. An establishment may be viewed "politically," in terms of the actions which each participant (or class of participants) can demand of other participants, the kinds of deprivations and indulgences which can be meted out in order to enforce these demands, and the kinds of social controls which guide this exercise of command and use of sanctions. An establishment may be viewed "structurally," in terms of the horizontal and vertical status divisions and the kinds of social relations which relate these several groupings to one another. Finally, an establishment may be viewed "culturally," in terms of the moral values which influence activity in the establishment—values pertaining to fashions, customs, and matters of taste, to politeness and decorum, to ultimate ends and normative restrictions on means, etc. It is to be noted that all the facts that can be discovered about an establishment are relevant to each of the four perspectives but that each perspective gives its own priority and order to these facts.

It seems to me that the dramaturgical approach may constitute a fifth perspective, to be added to the technical, political, structural, and cultural perspectives.[1] The dramaturgical perspective, like each of the other four, can be employed as the end-point of analysis, as a final way of ordering facts. This would lead us to describe the techniques of impression management employed

[1] Compare the position taken by Oswald Hall in regard to possible perspectives for the study of closed systems in his "Methods and Techniques of Research in Human Relations" (April, 1952), reported in E. C. Hughes et. al., *Cases on Field Work* (forthcoming)

in a given establishment, the principal problems of impression management in the establishment, and the identity and interrelationships of the several performance teams which operate in the establishment. But, as with the facts utilized in each of the other perspectives, the facts specifically pertaining to impression management also play a part in the matters that are a concern in all the other perspectives. It may be useful to illustrate this briefly.

The technical and dramaturgical perspectives intersect most clearly, perhaps, in regard to standards of work. Important for both perspectives is the fact that one set of individuals will be concerned with testing the unapparent characteristics and qualities of the work-accomplishments of another set of individuals, and this other set will be concerned with giving the impression that their work embodies these hidden attributes. The political and dramaturgical perspectives intersect clearly in regard to the capacities of one individual to direct the activity of another. For one thing, if an individual is to direct others, he will often find it useful to keep strategic secrets from them. Further, if one individual attempts to direct the activity of others by means of example, enlightenment, persuasion, exchange, manipulation, authority, threat, punishment, or coercion, it will be necessary, regardless of his power position, to convey effectively what he wants done, what he is prepared to do to get it done and what he will do if it is not done. Power of any kind must be clothed in effective means of displaying it, and will have different effects depending upon how it is dramatized. (Of course, the capacity to convey effectively a definition of the situation may be of little use if one is not in a position to give example, exchange, punishment, etc.) Thus the most objective form of naked power, i.e., physical coercion, is often neither objective nor naked but rather functions as a display for persuading the audience; it is often a means of communication, not merely a means of action. The structural and dramaturgical perspectives seem to intersect most clearly in regard to social distance. The image that one status grouping is able to maintain in the eyes of an audience of other status groupings will depend upon the performers' capacity to restrict communicative contact with the audience. The cultural and dramaturgical perspectives intersect most clearly in regard to the maintenance of moral standards. The cultural values of an establishment will determine in detail how the participants are to feel about many matters and at the same time establish a framework of appearances that must be maintained, whether or not there is feeling behind the appearances.

Personality-Interaction-Society

In recent years there have been elaborate attempts to bring into one framework the concepts and findings derived from three different areas of inquiry: the individual personality, social interaction, and society. I would like to suggest here a simple addition to these inter-disciplinary attempts.

When an individual appears before others, he knowingly and unwittingly projects a definition of the situation, of which a conception of himself is an important part. When an event occurs which is expressively incompatible with this fostered impression, significant consequences are simultaneously felt in three levels of social reality, each of which involves a different point of reference and a different order of fact.

First, the social interaction, treated here as a dialogue between two teams, may come to an embarrassed and confused halt; the situation may cease to be defined, previous positions may become no longer tenable, and participants may find themselves without a charted course of action. The participants typically sense a false note in the situation and come to feel awkward, flustered, and, literally, out of countenance. In other words, the minute social system created and sustained by orderly social interaction becomes disorganized. These are the consequences that the disruption has from the point of view of social interaction.

Secondly, in addition to these disorganizing consequences for action at the moment, performance disruptions may have consequences of a more far-reaching kind. Audiences tend to accept the self projected by the individual performer during any current performance as a responsible representative of his colleague-grouping, of his team, and of his social establishment. Audiences also accept the individual's particular performance as evidence of his capacity to perform the routine and even as evidence of his capacity to perform any routine. In a sense these larger social units—teams, establishments, etc.—become committed every time the individual performs his routine; with each performance the legitimacy of these units will tend to be tested anew and their permanent reputation put at stake. This kind of commitment is especially strong during some performances. Thus, when a surgeon and his nurse both turn from the operating table and the anesthetized patient accidentally rolls off the table to his death, not only is the operation disrupted in an embarrassing way, but the reputation of the doctor, as a doctor and as a man, and also the reputation of the hospital may be weakened. These are the consequences that disruptions may have from the point of view of social structure.

Finally, we often find that the individual may deeply involve his ego in his identification with a particular part, establishment, and group, and in his self-conception as someone who does not disrupt social interaction or let down the social units which depend upon that interaction. When a disruption occurs, then, we may find that the self-conceptions around which his personality has been built may become discredited. These are consequences that disruptions may have from the point of view of individual personality.

Performance disruptions, then, have consequences at three levels of abstraction: personality, interaction, and social structure. While the likelihood of disruption will vary widely from interaction to interaction, and while the social importance of likely disruptions will vary from interaction to interaction, still it seems that there is no interaction in which the participants do not take an appreciable chance of being slightly embarrassed or a slight chance of being deeply humiliated. Life may not be much of a gamble, but interaction is. Further, in so far as individuals make efforts to avoid disruptions or to correct for ones not avoided, these efforts, too, will have simultaneous consequences at the three levels. Here, then, we have one simple way of articulating three levels of abstraction and three perspectives from which social life has been studied.

Comparisons and Study

In this report, use has been made of illustrations from societies other than our Anglo-American one. In doing this I did not mean to imply that the framework presented here is culture-free or applicable in the same areas of social life in non-Western societies as in our own. We lead an indoor social life. We specialize in fixed settings, in keeping strangers out, and in giving the performer some privacy in which to prepare himself for the show. Once we begin a performance, we are inclined to finish it, and we are sensitive to jarring notes which may occur during it. If we are caught out in a misrepresentation we feel deeply humiliated. Given our general dramaturgical rules and inclinations for conducting action, we must not overlook areas of life in other societies in which other rules are apparently followed. Reports by Western travelers are filled with instances in which their dramaturgical sense was offended or surprised, and if we are to generalize to other cultures we must consider these instances as well as more favorable ones. We must be ready to see in China that while actions and décor may be wonderfully harmonious and coherent in a private tearoom, extremely elaborate meals may be served in extremely plain restaurants, and shops that look like hovels staffed with surly, familiar clerks may contain within their recesses, wrapped in old brown paper, wonderfully delicate bolts of silk.[1] And among a people said to be careful to save each other's face, we must be prepared to read that:

> Fortunately the Chinese do not believe in the privacy of a home as we do. They do not mind having the whole details of their daily experience seen by everyone that cares to look. How they live, what they eat, and even the family jars that we try to hush up from the public are things that seem to be common property, and not to belong exclusively to this particular family who are most concerned.[2]

And we must be prepared to see that in societies with settled inequalitarian status systems and strong religious orientations, individuals are sometimes less earnest about the whole civic drama than we are, and will cross social barriers with brief gestures that give more recognition to the man behind the mask than we might find permissible.

Furthermore, we must be very cautious in any effort to characterize our own society as a whole with respect to dramaturgical practices. For example, in current management-labor relations, we know that a team may enter joint consultation meetings with the opposition with the knowledge that it may be necessary to give the appearance of stalking out of the meeting in a huff. Diplomatic teams are sometimes required to stage a similar show. In other words, While teams in our society are usually obliged to suppress their rage behind a working consensus, there are times when teams are obliged to sup-

[1] Macgowan, J. Sidelights on Chinese Life (Philadelphia. Lippincott, 1908).
[2] *Ibid.*, pp. 180–81.

press the appearance of sober opposition behind a demonstration of outraged feelings. Similarly, there are occasions when individuals, whether they wish to or not, will feel obliged to destroy an interaction in order to save their honor and their face. It would be more prudent, then, to begin with smaller units, with social establishments or classes of establishments, or with particular statuses, and document comparisons and changes in a modest way by means of the case-history method. For example, we have the following kind of information about the shows that businessmen are legally allowed to put on:

> The last half-century has seen a marked change in the attitude of the courts toward the question of justifiable reliance. Earlier decisions, under the influence of the prevalent doctrine of "caveat emptor," laid great stress upon the plaintiff's "duty" to protect himself and distrust his antagonist, and held that he was not entitled to rely even upon positive assertions of fact made by one with whom he was dealing at arm's length. It was assumed that anyone may be expected to overreach another in a bargain if he can, and that only a fool will expect common honesty. Therefore the plaintiff must make a reasonable investigation, and form his own judgment. The recognition of a new standard of business ethics, demanding that statements of fact be at least honestly and carefully made, and in many cases that they be warranted to be true, has led to an almost complete shift in this point of view.
>
> It is now held that assertions of fact as to the quantity or quality of land or goods sold, the financial status of the corporations, and similar matters inducing commercial transactions, may justifiably be relied on without investigation, not only where such investigation would be burdensome and difficult, as where land which is sold lies at a distance, but likewise where the falsity of the representation might be discovered with little effort by means easily at hand.[3]

And while frankness may be increasing in business relations, we have some evidence that marriage counselors are increasingly agreed that an individual ought not to feel obliged to tell his or her spouse about previous "affairs," as this might only lead to needless strain. Other examples may be cited. We know, for example, that up to about 1830 pubs in Britain provided a backstage setting for workmen, little distinguishable from their own kitchens, and that after that date the gin palace suddenly burst upon the scene to provide much the same clientele with a fancier front region than they could dream of.[4] We have records of the social history of particular American towns, telling us of the recent decline in the elaborateness of domestic and avocational fronts of the local upper classes. In contrast, some material is available which describes the recent increase in elaborateness of the setting that union organizations employ,[5] and the increasing

---

[3] Prosser, William L., *Handbook of the Law of Torts*. (St. Paul, Minnesota, West Publishing, 1941), pp. 749–50.

[4] M. Gorham and H. Dunnett, *Inside the Pub* (London: The Architectural Press, 1950), pp. 23-24.

[5] See, for example, Floyd Hunter, *Community Power Structure* (Chapel Hill: University of North Carolina Press, 1953), p. 19.

tendency to "stock" the setting with academically-trained experts who provide an aura of thought and respectability.[6] We can trace changes in the plant layout of specific industrial and commercial organizations and show an increase in front, both as regards the exterior of the head-office building and as regards the conference rooms, main halls, and waiting rooms of these buildings. We can trace in a particular crofting community how the barn for animals, once backstage to the kitchen and accessible by a small door next the stove, has lately been removed a distance from the house, and how the house itself, once set down in an unprotected way in the midst of garden, croft equipment, garbage, and grazing stock, is becoming, in a sense, public-relations oriented, with a front yard fenced off and kept somewhat clean, presenting a dressed-up side to the community while debris is strewn at random in the unfenced back regions. And as the connected byre disappears, and the scullery itself starts to become less frequent, we can observe the up-grading of domestic establishments, wherein the kitchen, which once possessed its own back regions, is now coming to be the least presentable region of the house while at the same time becoming more and more presentable. We can also trace that peculiar social movement which led some factories, ships, restaurants, and households to clean up their backstages to such an extent that, like monks, Communists, or German aldermen, their guards are always up and there is no place where their front is down, while at the same time members of the audience become sufficiently entranced with the society's id to explore the places that had been cleaned up for them. Paid attendance at symphony orchestra rehearsals is only one of the latest examples. We can observe what Everett Hughes calls collective mobility, through which the occupants of a status attempt to alter the bundle of tasks performed by them so that no act will be required which is expressively inconsistent with the image of self that these incumbents are attempting to establish for themselves. And we can observe a parallel process, which might be called "role enterprise," within a particular social establishment, whereby a particular member attempts not so much to move into a higher position already established as to create a new position for himself, a position involving duties which suitably express attributes that are congenial to him. We can examine the process of specialization, whereby many performers come to make brief communal use of very elaborate social settings, being content to sleep alone in a cubicle of no pretension. We can follow the diffusion of crucial fronts—such as the laboratory complex of glass, stainless steel, rubber gloves, white tile, and lab coat—which allow an increasing number of persons connected with unseemly tasks a way of self-purification. Starting with the tendency in highly authoritarian organizations for one team to be required to spend its time infusing a rigorously ordered cleanliness in the setting the other team will perform in, we can trace, in establishments such as hospitals, air force bases, and large households, a current decline in the hypertrophic strictness of such settings. And finally, we can follow the rise and diffusion of the jazz and "West Coast" cultural patterns, in which terms such as bit, goof, scene, drag, dig, are given currency, allowing individuals to maintain something

[6] See Wilensky, *op. cit.*, chap. iv, for a discussion of the "window-dressing" function of staff experts.

of a professional stage performer's relation to the technical aspects of daily performances.

The Role of Expression Is Conveying Impressions of Self

Perhaps a moral note can be permitted at the end. In this report the expressive component of social life has been treated as a source of impressions given to or taken by others. Impression, in turn, has been treated as a source of information about unapparent facts and as a means by which the recipients can guide their response to the informant without having to wait for the full consequences of the informant's actions to be felt. Expression, then, has been treated in terms of the communicative role it plays during social interaction and not, for example, in terms of consummatory or tension-release function it might have for the expresser.[1]

Underlying all social interaction there seems to be a fundamental dialectic. When one individual enters the presence of others, he will want to discover the facts of the situation. Were he to possess this information, he could know, and make allowances for, what will come to happen and he could give the others present as much of their due as is consistent with his enlightened self-interest. To uncover fully the factual nature of the situation, it would be necessary for the individual to know all the relevant social data about the others. It would also be necessary for the individual to know the actual outcome or end product of the activity of the others during the interaction, as well as their innermost feelings concerning him. Full information of this order is rarely available; in its absence, the individual tends to employ substitutes—cues, tests, hints, expressive gestures, status symbols, etc.—as predictive devices. In short, since the reality that the individual is concerned with is unperceivable at the moment, appearances must be relied upon in its stead. And, paradoxically, the more the individual is concerned with the reality that is not available to perception, the more must he concentrate his attention on appearances.

The individual tends to treat the others present on the basis of the impression they give now about the past and the future. It is here that communicative acts are translated into moral ones. The impressions that the others give tend to be treated as claims and promises they have implicitly made, and claims and promises tend to have a moral character. In his mind the individual says: "I am using these impressions of you as a way of checking up on you and your activity, and you ought not to lead me astray." The peculiar thing about this is that the individual tends to take this stand even though he expects the others to be unconscious of many of their expressive behaviors and even though he may expect to exploit the others on the basis of the information he gleans about them. Since the sources of impression used by the observing individual involve a multitude of standards pertaining to politeness and decorum, pertaining both to

[1] A recent treatment of this kind may be found in Talcott Parsons, Robert F. Bales, and Edward A. Shils, *Working Papers in the Theory of Action* (Glencoe, Ill.: The Free Press, 1953), Chap. II, "The Theory of Symbolism in Relation to Action."

social intercourse and task-performance, we can appreciate afresh how daily life is enmeshed in moral lines of discrimination.

Let us shift now to the point of view of the others. If they are to be gentlemanly, and play the individual's game, they will give little conscious heed to the fact that impressions are being formed about them but rather act without guile or contrivance, enabling the individual to receive valid impressions about them and their efforts. And if they happen to give thought to the fact that they are being observed, they will not allow this to influence them unduly, content in the belief that the individual will obtain a correct impression and give them their due because of it. Should they be concerned with influencing the treatment that the individual gives them, and this is properly to be expected, then a gentlemanly means will be available to them. They need only guide their action in the present so that its future consequences will be the kind that would lead a just individual to treat them now in a way they want to be treated; once this is done, they have only to rely on the perceptiveness and justness of the individual who observes them.

Sometimes those who are observed do, of course, employ these proper means of influencing the way in which the observer treats them. But there is another way, a shorter and more efficient way, in which the observed can influence the observer. Instead of allowing an impression of their activity to arise as an incidental by-product of their activity, they can reorient their frame of reference and devote their efforts to the creation of desired impressions. Instead of attempting to achieve certain ends by acceptable means, they can attempt to achieve the impression that they are achieving certain ends by acceptable means. It is always possible to manipulate the impression the observer uses as a substitute for reality because a sign for the presence of a thing, not being that thing, can be employed in the absence of it. The observer's need to rely on representations of things itself creates the possibility of misrepresentation.

There are many sets of persons who feel they could not stay in business, whatever their business, if they limited themselves to the gentlemanly means of influencing the individual who observes them. At some point or other in the round of their activity they feel it is necessary to band together and directly manipulate the impression that they give. The observed become a performing team and the observers become the audience. Actions which appear to be done on objects become gestures addressed to the audience. The round of activity becomes dramatized.

We come now to the basic dialectic. In their capacity as performers, individuals will be concerned with maintaining the impression that they are living up to the many standards by which they and their products are judged. Because these standards are so numerous and so pervasive, the individuals who are performers dwell more than we might think in a moral world. But, *qua* performers, individuals are concerned not with the moral issue of realizing these standards, but with the amoral issue of engineering a convincing impression that these standards are being realized. Our activity, then, is largely concerned with moral matters, but as performers we do not have a moral concern with them. As performers we are merchants of morality. Our day is given over to intimate contact with the goods we display and our minds are filled with intimate understandings of them; but it may well be that the more attention we give to these goods, then the more distant we feel from them and from those who are believing enough to buy them. To use a different imagery, the very obligation and profitability of appearing always in a steady moral light, of being a socialized character, forces one to be the sort of person who is practiced in the ways of the stage.

Staging and the Self

The general notion that we make a presentation of ourselves to others is hardly novel; what ought to be stressed in conclusion is that the very structure of the self can be seen in terms of how we arrange for such performances in our Anglo-American society.

In this report, the individual was divided by implication into two basic parts: he was viewed as a *performer*, a harried fabricator of impressions involved in the all-too-human task of staging a performance; he was viewed as a *character*, a figure, typically a fine one, whose spirit, strength, and other sterling qualities the performance was designed to evoke. The attributes of a performer and the attributes of a character are of a different order, quite basically so, yet both sets have their meaning in terms of the show that must go on.

First, character. In our society the character one performs and one's self are somewhat equated, and this self-as-character is usually seen as something housed within the body of its possessor, especially the upper parts thereof, being a nodule, somehow, in the psychobiology of personality. I suggest that this view is an implied part of what we are all trying to present, but provides, just because of this, a bad analysis of the presentation. In this report the performed self was seen as some kind of image, usually creditable, which the individual on stage and in character effectively attempts to induce others to hold in regard to him. While this image is entertained *concerning* the individual, so that a self is imputed to him, this self itself does not derive from its possessor, but from the whole scene of his action, being generated by that attribute of local events which renders them interpretable by witnesses. A correctly staged and performed scene leads the audience to impute a self to a performed character, but this imputation—this self—is a *product* of a scene that comes off, and is not a *cause* of it. The self, then, as a performed character, is not an organic thing that has a specific location, whose fundamental fate is to be born, to mature, and to die; it is a dramatic effect arising diffusely from a scene that is presented, and the characteristic issue, the crucial concern, is whether it will be credited or discredited.

In analyzing the self then we are drawn from its possessor, from the person who will profit or lose most by it, for he and his body merely provide the peg on which something of collaborative manufacture will be hung for a time. And the means for producing and maintaining selves do not reside inside the peg; in fact these means are often bolted down in social establishments. There will be a back region with its tools for shaping the body, and a front region with its fixed props. There will be a team of persons whose activity on stage in conjunction with available props will constitute the scene from which the performed character's self will emerge, and another team, the audience, whose interpretive activity will be necessary for this emergence. The self is a product of all of these arrangements, and in all of its parts bears the marks of this genesis.

The whole machinery of self-production is cumbersome, of course, and sometimes breaks down, exposing its separate components: back region control; team collusion; audience tact; and so forth. But, well oiled, impressions will flow from it fast enough to put us in the grips of one of our types of reality—the performance will come off and the firm self accorded each performed character will appear to emanate intrinsically from its performer.

Let us turn now from the individual as character performed to the individual as performer. He has a capacity to learn, this being exercised in the task of training for a part. He is given to having fantasies and dreams, some that pleasurably unfold a triumphant performance, others full of anxiety and dread that nervously deal with vital discreditings in a public front region. He often manifests a gregarious desire for teammates and audiences, a tactful considerateness for their concerns; and he has a capacity for deeply felt shame, leading him to minimize the chances he takes of exposure.

These attributes of the individual *qua* performer are not merely a depicted effect of particular performances; they are psychobiological in nature, and yet they seem to arise out of intimate interaction with the contingencies of staging performances.

And now a final comment. In developing the conceptual framework employed in this report, some language of the stage was used. I spoke of performers and audiences; of routines and parts; of performances coming off or falling flat; of cues, stage settings and backstage; of dramaturgical needs, dramaturgical skills, and dramaturgical strategies. Now it should be admitted that this attempt to press a mere analogy so far was in part a rhetoric and a maneuver.

The claim that all the world's stage is sufficiently commonplace for readers to be familiar with its limitations and tolerant of its presentation, knowing that at any time they will easily be able to demonstrate to themselves that it is not to be taken too seriously. An action staged in a theater is a relatively contrived illusion and an admitted one; unlike ordinary life, nothing real or actual can happen to the performed characters—although at another level of course something real and actual can happen to the reputation of performers *qua* professionals whose everyday job is to put on theatrical performances.

And so here the language and mask of the stage will be dropped. Scaffolds, after all, are to build other things with, and should be erected with an eye to taking them down. This report is not concerned with aspects of theater that creep into everyday life. It is concerned with the structure of social encounters—the structure of those entities in social life that come into being whenever persons enter one another's immediate physical presence. The key factor in this structure is the maintenance of a single definition of the situation, this definition having to be expressed, and this expression sustained in the face of a multitude of potential disruptions.

A character staged in a theater is not in some ways real, nor does it have the same kind of real consequences as does the thoroughly contrived character performed by a confidence man; but the *successful* staging of either of these types of false figures involves use of *real* techniques—the same techniques by which everyday persons sustain their real social situations. Those who conduct face to face interaction on a theater's stage must meet the key requirement of real situations; they must expressively sustain a definition of the situation: but this they do in circumstances that have facilitated their developing an apt terminology for the interactional tasks that all of us share.

Although trained as a social anthropologist, Horace Miner (1912–1993) wrote one of the most recognized essays in sociology, *Body Ritual among the Nacirema*. Miner observes that the culture of the Nacirema regards the body as something to be manipulated and changed, while other bodily activities are to be hidden from view. Treatments for the body are kept in a special box in a home's shrine where most of the rituals aimed at changing, hiding, or otherwise treating the body take place. Miner's description of the strange, "magic-ridden" ways of the Nacirema shows how norms and cultural rituals govern aspects of everyday life and routine activities.

Body Ritual among the Nacirema

Horace Miner

The anthropologist has become so familiar with the diversity of ways in which different peoples behave in similar situations that he is not apt to be surprised by even the most exotic customs. In fact, if all of the logically possible combinations of behavior have not been found somewhere in the world, he is apt to suspect that they must be present in some yet undescribed tribe. This point has, in fact, been expressed with respect to clan organization by Murdock (1949:71). In this light, the magical beliefs and practices of the Nacirema present such unusual aspects that it seems desirable to describe them as an example of the extremes to which human behavior can go.

Professor Linton first brought the ritual of the Nacirema to the attention of anthropologists twenty years ago (1936:326), but the culture of this people is still very poorly understood. They are a North American group living in the territory between the Canadian Cree, the Yaqui and Tarahumare of Mexico, and the Carib and Arawak of the Antilles. Little is known of their origin, although tradition states that they came from the east. According to Nacirema mythology, their nation was originated by a culture hero, Notgnihsaw, who is otherwise known for two great feats of strength—the throwing of a piece of wampum across the river Pa-To-Mac and the chopping down of a cherry tree in which the Spirit of Truth resided.

Nacirema culture is characterized by a highly developed market economy which has evolved in a rich natural habitat. While much of the people's time is devoted to economic pursuits, a large part of the fruits of these labors and a considerable portion of the day are spent in ritual activity. The focus of this activity is the human body, the appearance and health of which loom as a dominant concern in the ethos of the people. While such a concern is certainly not unusual, its ceremonial aspects and associated philosophy are unique.

The fundamental belief underlying the whole system appears to be that the human body is ugly and that its natural tendency is to debility and disease. Incarcerated in such a body, man's only hope is to avert these characteristics through the use of the powerful influences of ritual and ceremony. Every household has one or more shrines devoted to this purpose. The more powerful individuals in the society have several shrines in their houses and, in fact, the opulence of a house is often referred to in terms of the number of such ritual centers it possesses. Most houses are of wattle and daub construction, but the shrine rooms of the more wealthy are walled with stone. Poorer families imitate the rich by applying pottery plaques to their shrine walls

While each family has at least one such shrine, the rituals associated with it are not family ceremonies but are private and secret. The rites are normally only discussed with children, and then only during the period when they are being initiated into these mysteries. I was able, however, to establish sufficient rapport with the natives to examine these shrines and to have the rituals described to me.

The focal point of the shrine is a box or chest which is built into the wall. In this chest are kept the many charms and magical potions without which no native believes he could live. These preparations are secured from a variety of specialized practitioners. The most powerful of these are the medicine men, whose assistance must be rewarded with substantial gifts. However, the medicine men do not provide the curative potions for their clients, but decide what the ingredients should be and then write them down in an ancient and secret language. This writing is understood only by the medicine men and by the herbalists who, for another gift, provide the required charm.

The charm is not disposed of after it has served its purpose, but is placed in the charm-box of the household shrine. As these magical materials are specific for certain ills, and the real or imagined maladies of the people are many, the charm-box is usually full to overflowing. The magical packets are so numerous that people forget what their purposes were and fear to use them again. While the natives are very vague on this point, we can only assume that the idea in retaining all the old magical materials is that their presence in the charm-box, before which the body rituals are conducted, will in some way protect the worshipper.

Beneath the charm-box is a small font. Each day every member of the family, in succession, enters the shrine room, bows his head before the charm-box, mingles different sorts of holy water in the font, and proceeds with a brief rite of ablution. The holy waters are secured from the Water Temple of the community, where the priests conduct elaborate ceremonies to make the liquid ritually pure.

In the hierarchy of magical practitioners, and below the medicine men in, prestige, are specialists whose designation is best translated "holy-mouth-men." The Nacirema have an almost pathological horror of and fascination with the mouth, the condition of which is believed to have a supernatural influence on all social relationships. Were it not for the rituals of the mouth, they believe that their teeth would fall out, their gums bleed, their jaws shrink, their friends desert them, and their lovers reject them. They also believe that a strong relationship exists between oral and moral characteristics. For example, there is a ritual ablution of the mouth for children which is supposed to improve their moral fiber.

The daily body ritual performed by everyone includes a mouth-rite. Despite the fact that these people are so punctilious about care of the mouth, this rite involves a practice which strikes the uninitiated stranger as revolting. It was reported to me that the ritual consists of inserting a small bundle of hog hairs into the mouth, along with certain magical powders, and then moving the bundle in a highly formalized series of gestures.

In addition to the private mouth-rite, the people seek out a holy-mouth-man once or twice a year. These practitioners have an impressive set of paraphernalia, consisting of a variety of augers, awls, probes, and prods. The use of these objects in the exorcism of the evils of the mouth involves almost unbelievable ritual torture of the client. The holy-mouth-man opens the client's mouth and, using the above mentioned tools, enlarges any holes which decay may have created in the teeth. Magical materials are put into these holes. If there are no naturally occurring holes in the teeth, large sections of one or more teeth are gouged out so that the supernatural substance can be applied. In the client's view, the purpose of these ministrations is to arrest decay and to draw friends. The extremely sacred and traditional character of the rite is evident in the fact that the natives return to the holy-mouth-men year after year, despite the fact that their teeth continue to decay.

It is to be hoped that, when a thorough study of the Nacirema is made, there will be careful inquiry into the personality structure of these people. One has but to watch the gleam in the eye of a holy-mouth-man, as he jabs an awl into an exposed nerve, to suspect that a certain amount of sadism is involved. If this can be established, a very interesting pattern emerges, for most of the population shows definite masochistic tendencies. It was to these that Professor Linton referred in discussing a distinctive part of the daily body ritual which is performed only by men. This part of the rite involves scraping and lacerating the surface of the face with a sharp instrument. Special women's rites are performed only four times during each lunar month, but what they lack in frequency is made up in barbarity. As part of this ceremony, women bake their heads in small ovens for about an hour. The theoretically interesting point is that what seems to be a preponderantly masochistic people have developed sadistic specialists.

The medicine men have an imposing temple, or *lalipso,* in every community of any size. The more elaborate ceremonies required to treat very sick patients can only be performed at this temple. These ceremonies involve not only the thaumaturge but a permanent group of vestal maidens who move sedately about the temple chambers in distinctive costume and headdress.

The *lalipso* ceremonies are so harsh that it is phenomenal that a fair proportion of the really sick natives who enter the temple ever recover. Small children whose indoctrination is still incomplete have been known to resist attempts to take them to the temple because "that is where you go to die." Despite this fact, sick adults are not only willing but eager to undergo the protracted ritual purification, if they can afford to do so. No matter how ill the supplicant or how grave the emergency, the guardians of many temples will not admit a client if he cannot give a rich gift to the custodian. Even after one has gained admission and survived the ceremonies, the guardians will not permit the neophyte to leave until he makes still another gift.

The supplicant entering the temple is first stripped of all his or her clothes. In every-day life the Nacirema avoids exposure of his body and its natural functions. Bathing and excretory acts are performed only in the secrecy of the household shrine, where they are ritualized as part of the body-rites. Psychological shock results from the fact that body secrecy is suddenly lost upon entry into the *lalipso*. A man, whose own wife has never seen him in an excretory act, suddenly finds himself naked and assisted by a vestal maiden while he performs his natural functions into a sacred vessel. This sort of ceremonial treatment is necessitated by the fact that the excreta are used by a diviner to ascertain the course and nature of the client's sickness. Female clients, on the other hand, find their naked bodies are subjected to the scrutiny, manipulation and prodding of the medicine men.

Few supplicants in the temple are well enough to do anything but lie on their hard beds. The daily ceremonies, like the rites of the holy-mouth-men, involve discomfort and torture. With ritual precision, the vestals awaken their miserable charges each dawn and roll them about on their beds of pain while performing ablutions, in the formal movements of which the maidens are highly trained. At other times they insert magic wands in the supplicant's mouth or force him to eat substances which are supposed to be healing. From time to time the medicine men come to their clients and jab magically treated needles into their flesh. The fact that these temple ceremonies may not cure and may even kill the neophyte in no way decreases the people's faith in the medicine men.

There remains one other kind of practitioner, known as a "listener." This witch-doctor has the power to exercise the devils that lodge in the heads of people who have been bewitched. The Nacirema believe that parents bewitch their own children. Mothers are particularly suspected of putting a curse on children while teaching them the secret body rituals. The counter-magic of the witch-doctor is unusual in its lack of ritual. The patient simply tells the "listener" all his troubles and fears, beginning with the earliest difficulties he can remember. The memory displayed by the Nacirema in these exorcism sessions is truly remarkable. It is not uncommon for the patient to bemoan the rejection he felt upon being weaned as a babe, and a few individuals even see their troubles going back to the traumatic effects of their own birth.

In conclusion, mention must be made of certain practices which have their base in native esthetics but which depend upon the pervasive aversion to the natural body and its functions. There are ritual fasts to make fat people thin and ceremonial feasts to make thin people fat. Still other rites are used to make women's breasts larger if they are small, and smaller if they are large. General dissatisfaction with breast shape is symbolized in the fact that the ideal form is virtually outside the range of human variation. A few women afflicted with almost inhuman hypermammary development are so idolized that they make a handsome living by simply going from village to village and permitting the natives to stare at them for a fee.

Reference has already been made to the fact that excretory functions are ritualized, routinized, and relegated to secrecy. Natural reproductive functions are similarly distorted. Intercourse is taboo as a topic and scheduled as an act. Efforts are made to avoid pregnancy by the use of magical materials or by limiting intercourse to certain phases of the moon. Conception is actually very infrequent. When pregnant, women dress so as to hide their condition. Parturition takes place in secret, without friends or relatives to assist, and the majority of women do not nurse their infants.

Our review of the ritual life of the Nacirema has certainly shown them to be a magic-ridden people. It is hard to understand how they have managed to exist so long under the burdens which they have imposed upon themselves. But even such exotic customs as these take on real meaning when they are viewed with the insight provided by Malinowski when he wrote (1948:70):

> Looking from far and above, from our high places of safety in the developed civilization, it is easy to see all the crudity and irrelevance of magic. But without its power and guidance early man could not have mastered his practical difficulties as he has done, nor could man have advanced to the higher stages of civilization.

References Cited:

Linton, Ralph. 1936. *The Study of Man*. New York, D. Appleton-Century Co.

Malinowski, Bronislaw. 1948. *Magic, Science, and Religion*. Glencoe, The Free Press.

Murdock, George P. 1949. *Social Structure*. New York, The Macmillan Co.

Jessie Bernard (1903–1996) had a long and productive career as a sociologist. In 1972 she produced a penetrating feminist analysis of the gender inequalities in marriage. In this book, *The Future of Marriage*, Bernard maintains that there are "his" and "her" marriages. Men benefit more from their marriage than women because they have more power, control, and freedom, which are explicitly supported by the state and the church. Keeping these structural inequalities in mind, Bernard is especially interested in how different, both in subjective and objective terms, the "wife's marriage has actually been from the husband's throughout history." This excerpt provides the groundwork for such an examination.

The Two Marriages

Jessie Bernard

The Future of Whose Marriage?

Both Uncle Honoré and Gigi's grandmother remembered it well, according to Alan Jay Lerner's lyric. And this is what it had been like according to Uncle Honoré: "it was a lovely moonlit evening in May. You arrived at nine o'clock in your gold dress only a little late for our dinner engagement with friends. Afterwards there was that delightful carriage ride when we were so engrossed in one another that we didn't notice you had lost your glove." Ah, yes, Uncle Honoré remembered it well indeed, down to the last detail.

Or, come to think of it, did he? For Gigi's grandmother remembered it too, but not at all the same way. "There was no moon that rainy June evening. For once I was on time when we met at eight o'clock at the restaurant where we dined alone. You complimented me on my pretty blue dress. Afterwards we took a long walk and we were so engrossed in one another that we didn't notice I had lost my comb until my hair came tumbling down."

The Japanese motion picture *Rashomon* was built on the same idea—four different versions of the same events. So, also, was Robert Gover's story of the college boy and the black prostitute in his *One Hundred Dollar Misunderstanding*. Also in this category is the old talmudic story of the learned rabbi called upon to render a decision in a marital situation. After listening carefully to the first spouse's story, he shook his head, saying, "You are absolutely right"; and, after listening equally carefully to the other spouse's story, he again shook his head, saying, "You are absolutely right."

There is no question in any of these examples of deliberate deceit or prevarication or insincerity or dishonesty. Both Uncle Honoré and Grandmamma are equally sincere, equally honest, equally "right." The discrepancies in their stories make a charming duet in *Gigi*. And even the happiest of mates can match such differences in their own memories.

In the case of Uncle Honoré and Grandmamma, we can explain the differences in the pictures they had in their heads of that evening half a century earlier: memories play strange tricks on all of us. But the same differences in the accounts of what happened show up also among modern couples even immediately after the event. In one study, for example, half of all the partners gave differing replies to questions about what had happened in a laboratory decision-making session they had just left. Other couples give different responses to questions about ordinary day-by-day events like lawn mowing as well as about romantic events. Once our attention has been called to the fact that both mates are equally sincere, equally honest, equally "right," the presence of two marriages in every marital union becomes clear—even obvious, as artists and wise persons have been telling us for so long.

Anyone, therefore, discussing the future of marriage has to specify whose marriage he is talking about: the husband's or the wife's. For there is by now a very considerable body of well-authenticated research to show that there really are two marriages in every marital union, and that they do not always coincide.

"His" and "Her" Marriages

Under the jargon "discrepant responses," the differences in the marriages of husbands and wives have come under the careful scrutiny of a score of researchers. They have found that when they ask husbands and wives identical questions about the union, they often get quite different replies. There is usually agreement on the number of children they have and a few other such verifiable items, although not, for example, on length of premarital acquaintance and of engagement, on age at marriage and interval between marriage and birth of first child. Indeed, with respect to even such basic components of the marriage as frequency of sexual relations, social interaction, household tasks, and decision making, they seem to be reporting on different marriages. As, I think, they are.

In the area of sexual relations, for example, Kinsey and his associates found different responses in from one- to two-thirds of the couples they studied. Kinsey interpreted these differences in terms of selective perception. In the generation he was studying, husbands wanted sexual relations oftener than the wives did, thus "the females may be overestimating the actual frequencies" and "the husbands . . . are probably underestimating the frequencies." The differences might also have been vestiges of the probable situation earlier in the marriage when the desired frequency of sexual relations was about six to seven times greater among husbands than among wives. This difference may have become so impressed on the spouses that it remained in their minds even after the difference itself had disappeared or even been reversed. In a sample of happily married, middle-class couples a generation later, Harold Feldman found that both spouses attributed to their mates more influence in the area of sex than they did to themselves.

Companionship, as reflected in talking together, he found, was another area where differences showed up. Replies differed on three-fourths of all the items studied, including the topics talked about, the amount of time spent talking with each other, and which partner initiated conversation. Both partners claimed that whereas they talked more about topics of interest to their mates, their mates initiated conversations about topics primarily of interest to themselves. Harold Feldman concluded that projection in terms of needs was distorting even simple, everyday events, and lack of communication was permitting the distortions to continue.[1] It seemed to him that "if these sex differences can occur so often among these generally well satisfied couples, it would not be surprising to find even less consensus and more distortion in other less satisfied couples."

Although, by and large, husbands and wives tend to become more alike with age, in this study of middle-class couples, differences increased with length of marriage rather than decreased, as one might logically have expected. More couples in the later than in the earlier years, for example, had differing pictures in their heads about how often they laughed together, discussed together, exchanged ideas, or worked together on projects, and about how well things were going between them.

The special nature of sex and the amorphousness of social interaction help to explain why differences in response might occur. But household tasks? They are fairly objective and clear-cut and not all that emotion-laden. Yet even here there are his-and-her versions. Since the division of labor in the household is becoming increasingly an issue in marriage, the uncovering of differing replies in this area is especially relevant. Hard as it is to believe, Granbois and Willett tell us that more than half of the partners in one sample disagreed on who kept track of money and bills. On the question, who mows the lawn? more than a fourth disagreed. Even family income was not universally agreed on.

These differences about sexual relations, companionship, and domestic duties tell us a great deal about the two marriages. But power or decision making can cover all aspects of a relationship. The question of who makes decisions or who exercises power has therefore attracted a great deal of research attention. If we were interested in who really had the power or who really made the decisions, the research would be hopeless. Would it be possible to draw any conclusion from a situation in which both partners agree that the husband ordered the wife to make all the decisions? Still, an enormous literature documents the quest of researchers for answers to the question of marital power. The major contribution it has made has been to reveal the existence of differences in replies between husbands and wives.

The presence of such inconsistent replies did not at first cause much concern. The researchers apologized for them but interpreted them as due to methodological inadequacies; if only they could find a better way to approach the problem, the differences would disappear. Alternatively, the use of only the wife's responses, which were more easily available, was justified on the grounds

---

[1] For a discussion of the part played by communication in all relations between the sexes, see Jessie Bernard, *The Sex Game* (Englewood Cliffs, NJ, Prentice-Hall, 1968; New York: Atheneum, 1972). Chapter 10 deals with communication in marriage.

that differences in one direction between the partners in one marriage compensated for differences in another direction between the partners in another marriage and thus canceled them out. As, indeed, they did. For when Granbois and Willett, two market researchers, analyzed the replies of husbands and wives separately, the overall picture was in fact the same for both wives and husbands. Such canceling out of differences in the total sample, however, concealed almost as much as it revealed about the individual couples who composed it. Granbois and Willett concluded, as Kinsey had earlier, that the "discrepancies . . . reflect differing perceptions on the part of responding partners." And this was the heart of the matter.

Differing reactions to common situations, it should be noted, are not at all uncommon. They are recognized in the folk wisdom embedded in the story of the blind men all giving different replies to questions on the nature of the elephant. One of the oldest experiments in juridical psychology demonstrates how different the statements of witnesses of the same act can be. Even in laboratory studies, it takes intensive training of raters to make it possible for them to arrive at agreement on the behavior they observe.

It has long been known that people with different backgrounds see things differently. We know, for example, that poor children perceive coins as larger than do children from more affluent homes. Boys and girls perceive differently. A good deal of the foundation for projective tests rests on the different ways in which individuals see identical stimuli. And this perception—or, as the sociologists put it, definition of the situation—is reality for them. In this sense, the realities of the husband's marriage are different from those of the wife's.

Finally, one of the most perceptive of the researchers, Constantina Safilios-Rothschild, asked the crucial question: Was what they were getting, even with the best research techniques, family sociology or wives' family sociology? She answered her own question: What the researchers who relied on wives' replies exclusively were reporting on was the wife's marriage. The husband's was not necessarily the same. There were, in fact, two marriages present:

> One explanation of discrepancies between the responses of husbands and wives may be the possibility of two "realities," the husband's subjective reality and the wife's subjective reality—two perspectives which do not always coincide. Each spouse perceives "facts" and situations differently according to his own needs, values, attitudes, and beliefs. An "objective" reality could possibly exist only in the trained observer's evaluation, if it does exist at all.

Interpreting the different replies of husbands and wives in terms of selective perception, projection of needs, values, attitudes, and beliefs, or different definitions of the situation, by no means renders them trivial or incidental or justifies dismissing or ignoring them. They are, rather, fundamental for an understanding of the two marriages, his and hers, and we ignore them at the peril of serious misunderstanding of marriage, present as well as future.

Is There an Objective Reality in Marriage?

Whether or not husbands and wives perceive differently or define situations differently, still sexual relations are taking place, companionship is or is not occurring, tasks about the house are being performed, and decisions are being made every day by someone. In this sense, some sort of "reality" does exist. David Olson went to the laboratory to see if he could uncover it.

He first asked young couples expecting babies such questions as these: Which one of them would decide whether to buy insurance for the newborn child? Which one would decide the husband's part in diaper changing? Which one would decide whether the new mother would return to work or to school? When there were differences in the answers each gave individually on the questionnaire, he set up a situation in which together they had to arrive at a decision in his laboratory. He could then compare the results of the questionnaire with the results in the simulated situation. He found neither spouse's questionnaire response any more accurate than the other's; that is, neither conformed better to the behavioral "reality" of the laboratory than the other did.

The most interesting thing, however, was that husbands, as shown on their questionnaire response, perceived themselves as having more power than they actually did have in the laboratory "reality," and wives perceived that they had less. Thus, whereas three-fourths (73 percent) of the husbands overestimated their power in decision making, 70 percent of the wives underestimated theirs. Turk and Bell found similar results in Canada. Both spouses tend to attribute decision-making power to the one who has the "right" to make the decision. Their replies, that is, conform to the model of marriage that has characterized civilized mankind for millennia. It is this model rather than their own actual behavior that husbands and wives tend to perceive.

We are now zeroing in on the basic reality. We can remove the quotation marks. For there is, in fact, an objective reality in marriage. It is a reality that resides in the cultural—legal, moral, and conventional—prescriptions and proscriptions and, hence, expectations that constitute marriage. It is the reality that is reflected in the minds of the spouses themselves. The differences between the marriages of husbands and of wives are structural realities, and it is these structural differences that constitute the basis for the different psychological realities.

The Authority Structure of Marriage

Authority is an institutional phenomenon; it is strongly bound up with faith. It must be believed in; it cannot be enforced unless it also has power. Authority resides not in the person on whom it is conferred by the group or society, but in the recognition and acceptance it elicits in others. Power, on the other hand, may dispense with the prop of authority. It may take the form of the ability to coerce or to veto; it is often personal, charismatic, not institutional. This kind of personal power is self-enforcing. It does not require shoring up by access to force. In fact, it may even operate subversively. A women with this kind of power may or may not know that she possesses it. If she does know she has it, she will probably disguise her exercise of it.

In the West, the institutional structure of marriage has invested the husband with authority and backed it by the power of church and state. The marriages of wives have thus been officially dominated by the husband. Hebrew, Christian, and Islamic versions of deity were in complete accord on this matter. The laws, written or unwritten, religious or civil, which have defined the marital union have been based on male conceptions, and they have undergirded male authority.

Adam came first. Eve was created to supply him with companionship, not vice versa. And God himself had told her that Adam would rule over her; her wishes had to conform to his. The New Testament authors agreed. Women were created for men, not men for women; women were therefore commanded to be obedient. If they wanted to learn anything, let them ask their husbands in private, for it was shameful for them to talk in the church. They should submit themselves to their husbands, because husbands were superior to wives; and wives should be as subject to their husbands as the church was to Christ. Timothy wrapped it all up: "Let the woman learn in silence with all subjection. But I suffer not a woman to teach, nor to usurp authority over the man, but to be in silence." Male Jews continued for millennia to thank God three times a day that they were not women. And the Koran teaches women that men are naturally their superiors because God made them that way; naturally, their own status is one of subordination.

The state as well as the church had the same conception of marriage, assigning to the husband and father control over his dependents, including his wife. Sometimes this power was well-nigh absolute, as in the case of the Roman patria potestas—or the English common law, which flatly said, "*The husband and wife are as one and that one is the husband.*" There are rules still lingering today with the same, though less extreme, slant. Diane B. Schulder has summarized the legal framework of the wife's marriage as laid down in the common law.

> The legal responsibilities of a wife are to live in the home established by her husband; to perform the domestic chores (cleaning, cooking, washing, etc.) necessary to help maintain that home; to care for her husband and children. . . . A husband may force his wife to have sexual relations as long as his demands are reasonable and her health is not endangered. . . . The law allows a wife to take a job if she wishes. However, she must see that her domestic chores are completed, and, if there are children, that they receive proper care during her absence.

A wife is not entitled to payment for household work; and some jurisdictions in the United States expressly deny payment for it. In some states, the wife's earnings are under the control of her husband, and in four, special court approval and in some cases husband's consent are required if a wife wishes to start a business of her own.

The male counterpart to these obligations includes that of supporting his wife. He may not disinherit her. She has a third interest in property owned by him, even if it is held in his name only. Her name is required when he sells property.

Not only divine and civil law but also rules of etiquette have defined authority as a husband's prerogative. One of the first books published in England was a *Boke of Good Manners*, translated from the French of Jacques Le Grand in 1487, which included a chapter on "How Wymmen Ought to Be Gouerned." The thirty-third rule of Plutarch's *Rules for Husbands and Wives* was that women should obey their husbands; if they "try to rule over their husbands they make a worse mistake than the husbands do who let themselves be ruled." The husband's rule should not, of course, be brutal; he should not rule his wife "as a master does his chattel, but as the soul governs the body, by feeling with her and being linked to her by affection." Wives, according to Richard Baxter, a seventeenth-century English divine, had to obey even a wicked husband, the only exception being that a wife need not obey a husband if he ordered her to change her religion. But, again, like Plutarch, Baxter warned that the husband should love his wife; his authority should not be so coercive or so harsh as to destroy love. Among his twelve rules for carrying out the duties of conjugal love, however, was one to the effect that love must not be so imprudent as to destroy authority.

As late as the nineteenth century, Tocqueville noted that in the United States the ideals of democracy did not apply between husbands and wives:

> Nor have the Americans ever supposed that one consequence of democratic principles is the subversion of marital power, or the confusion of the natural authorities in families. They hold that every association must have a head in order to accomplish its objective, and that the natural head of the conjugal association is man. They do not therefore deny him the right of directing his partner; and they maintain, that in the smaller association of husband and wife, as well as in the great social community, the object of democracy is to regulate and legalize the powers which are necessary, not to subvert all power.
>
> This opinion is not peculiar to men and contested by women; I never observed that the women of America consider conjugal authority as a fortunate usurpation [by men] of their rights, nor that they thought themselves degraded by submitting to it. It appears to me, on the contrary, that they attach a sort of pride to the voluntary surrender of their own will, and make it their boast to bend themselves to the yoke, not to shake it off.

The point here is not to document once more the specific ways (religious, legal, moral, traditional) in which male authority has been built into the marital union—that has been done a great many times—but merely to illustrate how different (structurally or "objectively" as well as perceptually or "subjectively") the wife's marriage has actually been from the husband's throughout history.

The Subversiveness of Nature

The rationale for male authority rested not only on biblical grounds but also on nature or natural law, on the generally accepted natural superiority of men. For nothing could be more self-evident than that the patriarchal conception of marriage, in which the husband was unequivocally the boss, was natural, resting as it did on the unchallenged superiority of males.

Actually, nature, if not deity, is subversive. Power, or the ability to coerce or to veto, is widely distributed in both sexes, among women as well as among men. And whatever the theoretical or conceptual picture may have been, the actual, day-by-day relationships between husbands and wives have been determined by the men and women themselves. All that the institutional machinery could do was to confer authority; it could not create personal power, for such power cannot be conferred, and women can generate it as well as men, a matter examined in greater detail in chapter 7. Thus, keeping women in their place has been a universal problem, in spite of the fact that almost without exception institutional patterns give men positions of superiority over them.

If the sexes were, in fact, categorically distinct, with no overlapping, so that no man was inferior to any woman or any woman superior to any man, or vice versa, marriage would have been a great deal simpler. But there is no such sharp cleavage between the sexes except with respect to the presence or absence of certain organs. With all the other characteristics of each sex, there is greater or less overlapping, some men being more "feminine" than the average woman and some women more "masculine" than the average man. The structure of families and societies reflects the positions assigned to men and women. The bottom stratum includes children, slaves, servants, and outcasts of all kinds, males as well as females. As one ascends the structural hierarchy, the proportion of males increases, so that at the apex there are only males.

When societies fall back on the lazy expedient—as all societies everywhere have done—of allocating the rewards and punishments of life on the basis of sex, they are bound to create a host of anomalies, square pegs in round holes, societal misfits. Roles have been allocated on the basis of sex which did not fit a sizable number of both sexes—women, for example, who chafed at subordinate status and men who could not master superordinate status. The history of the relations of the sexes is replete with examples of such misfits. Unless a modus vivendi is arrived at, unhappy marriages are the result.

There is, though, a difference between the exercise of power by husbands and by wives. When women exert power, they are not rewarded; they may even be punished. They are "deviant." Turk and Bell note that "wives who . . . have the greater influence in decision making may experience guilt over this fact." They must therefore dissemble to maintain the illusion, even to themselves, that they are subservient. They tend to feel less powerful than they are because they *ought* to be.

When men exert power, on the other hand, they are rewarded; it is the natural expression of authority. They feel no guilt about it. The prestige of authority goes to the husband whether or not he is actually the one who exercises it. It is not often even noticed when the wife does so. She sees to it that it is not.

There are two marriages, then, in every marital union, his and hers. And his, is better than hers. The questions, therefore, are these: In what direction will they change in the future? Will one change more than the other? Will they tend to converge or to diverge? Will the future continue to favor the husband's marriage? And if the wife's marriage is improved, will it cost the husband's anything, or will his benefit along with hers?

Maverick sociologist and social critic C. Wright Mills produced the influential book *The Power Elite* in 1956, six years before his death. The power elite, according to Mills, is composed of men who occupy positions of authority in major institutions and organizations in the economic, political, and military arenas. These men are wealthy, have prestigious jobs, and wield extraordinary decision making powers. Even their decisions not to act can be influential. The concentration of wealth and power into the hands of the few is especially noteworthy, according to Mills, as economic, political, and military institutions are more connected than separate.

The Power Elite

C. Wright Mills

The powers of ordinary men are circumscribed by the everyday worlds in which they live, yet even in these rounds of job, family, and neighborhood they often seem driven by forces they can neither understand nor govern. 'Great changes' are beyond their control, but affect their conduct and outlook none the less. The very framework of modern society confines them to projects not their own, but from every side, such changes now press upon the men and women of the mass society, who accordingly feel that they are without purpose in an epoch in which they are without power.

But not all men are in this sense ordinary. As the means of information and of power are centralized, some men come to occupy positions in American society from which they can look down upon, so to speak, and by their decisions mightily affect, the everyday worlds of ordinary men and women. They are not made by their jobs; they set up and break down jobs for thousands of others; they are not confined by simple family responsibilities; they can escape. They may live in many hotels and houses, but they are bound by no one community. They need not merely 'meet the demands of the day and hour'; in some part, they create these demands, and cause others to meet them. Whether or not they profess their power, their technical and political experience of it far transcends that of the underlying population. (What Jacob Burckhardt said of 'great men,' most Americans might well say of their elite: 'They are all that we are not.')[1]

The power elite is composed of men whose positions enable them to transcend the ordinary environments of ordinary men and women; they are in positions to make decisions having major consequences. Whether they do or do not make such decisions is less important than the fact that they do occupy such pivotal positions: their failure to act, their failure to make decisions, is itself an act that is often of greater consequence than the decisions they do make. For they are in command of the major hierarchies and organizations of modern society.

[1] Jacob Burckhardt, *Force and Freedom* (New York: Pantheon Books, 1943), pp. 303ff.

They rule the big corporations. They run the machinery of the state and claim its prerogatives. They direct the military establishment. They occupy the strategic command posts of the social structure, in which are now centered the effective means of the power and the wealth and the celebrity which they enjoy.

The power elite are not solitary rulers. Advisers and consultants, spokesmen and opinion-makers are often the captains of their higher thought and decision. Immediately below the elite are the professional politicians of the middle levels of power, in the Congress and in the pressure groups, as well as among the new and old upper classes of town and city and region. Mingling with them, in curious ways which we shall explore, are those professional celebrities who live by being continually displayed but are never, so long as they remain celebrities, displayed enough. If such celebrities are not at the head of any dominating hierarchy, they do often have the power to distract the attention of the public or afford sensations to the masses, or, more directly, to gain the ear of those who do occupy positions of direct power. More or less unattached, as critics of morality and technicians of power, as spokesmen of God and creators of mass sensibility, such celebrities and consultants are part of the immediate scene in which the drama of the elite is enacted. But that drama itself is centered in the command posts of the major institutional hierarchies.

1

The truth about the nature and the power of the elite is not some secret which men of affairs know but will not tell. Such men hold quite various theories about their own roles in the sequence of event and decision. Often they are uncertain about their roles, and even more often they allow their fears and their hopes to affect their assessment of their own power. No matter how great their actual power, they tend to be less acutely aware of it than of the resistances of others to its use. Moreover, most American men of affairs have learned well the rhetoric of public relations, in some cases even to the point of using it when they are alone, and thus coming to believe it. The personal awareness of the actors is only one of the several sources one must examine in order to understand the higher circles. Yet many who believe that there is no elite, or at any rate none of any consequence, rest their argument upon what men of affairs believe about themselves, or at least assert in public.

There is, however, another view: those who feel, even if vaguely, that a compact and powerful elite of great importance does now prevail in America often base that feeling upon the historical trend of our time. They have felt, for example, the domination of the military event, and from this they infer that generals and admirals, as well as other men of decision influenced by them, must be enormously powerful. They hear that the Congress has again abdicated to a handful of men decisions clearly related to the issue of war or peace. They know that the bomb was dropped over Japan in the name of the United States of America, although they were at no time consulted about the matter.

They feel that they live in a time of big decisions; they know that they are not making any. Accordingly, as they consider the present as history, they infer that at its center, making decisions or failing to make them, there must be an elite of power.

On the one hand, those who share this feeling about big historical events assume that there is an elite and that its power is great. On the other hand, those who listen carefully to the reports of men apparently involved in the great decisions often do not believe that there is an elite whose powers are of decisive consequence.

Both views must be taken into account, but neither is adequate. The way to understand the power of the American elite lies neither solely in recognizing the historic scale of events nor in accepting the personal awareness reported by men of apparent decision. Behind such men and behind the events of history, linking the two, are the major institutions of modern society. These hierarchies of state and corporation and army constitute the means of power; as such they are now of a consequence not before equaled in human history—and at their summits, there are now those command posts of modern society which offer us the sociological key to an understanding of the role of the higher circles in America.

Within American society, major national power now resides in the economic, the political, and the military domains. Other institutions seem off to the side of modern history, and, on occasion, duly subordinated to these. No family is as directly powerful in national affairs as any major corporation; no church is as directly powerful in the external biographies of young men in America today as the military establishment; no college is as powerful in the shaping of momentous events as the National Security Council. Religious, educational, and family institutions are not autonomous centers of national power; on the contrary, these decentralized areas are increasingly shaped by the big three, in which developments of decisive and immediate consequence now occur.

Families and churches and schools adapt to modern life; governments and armies and corporations shape it; and, as they do so, they turn these lesser institutions into means for their ends. Religious institutions provide chaplains to the armed forces where they are used as a means of increasing the effectiveness of its morale to kill. Schools select and train men for their jobs in corporations and their specialized tasks in the armed forces. The extended family has, of course, long been broken up by the industrial revolution, and now the son and the father are removed from the family, by compulsion if need be, whenever the army of the state sends out the call. And the symbols of all these lesser institutions are used to legitimate the power and the decisions of the big three.

The life-fate of the modern individual depends not only upon the family into which he was born or which he enters by marriage, but increasingly upon the corporation in which he spends the most alert hours of his best years; not only upon the school where he is educated as a child and adolescent, but also upon the state which touches him throughout his life; not only upon the church in which on occasion he hears the word of God, but also upon the army in which he is disciplined.

If the centralized state could not rely upon the inculcation of nationalist loyalties in public and private schools, its leaders would promptly seek to modify the decentralized educational system. If the bankruptcy rate among the top five hundred corporations were as high as the general divorce rate among the thirty-seven million married couples, there would be economic catastrophe on an international scale. If members of armies gave to them no more of their lives than do believers to the churches to which they belong, there would be a military crisis.

Within each of the big three, the typical institutional unit has become enlarged, has become administrative, and, in the power of its decisions, has become centralized. Behind these developments there is a fabulous technology, for as institutions, they have incorporated this technology and guide it, even as it shapes and paces their developments.

The economy—once a great scatter of small productive units in autonomous balance—has become dominated by two or three hundred giant corporations, administratively and politically interrelated, which together hold the keys to economic decisions.

The political order, once a decentralized set of several dozen states with a weak spinal cord, has become a centralized, executive establishment which has taken up into itself many powers previously scattered, and now enters into each and every crany of the social structure.

The military order, once a slim establishment in a context of distrust fed by state militia, has become the largest and most expensive feature of government, and, although well versed in smiling public relations, now has all the grim and clumsy efficiency of a sprawling bureaucratic domain.

In each of these institutional areas, the means of power at the disposal of decision makers have increased enormously; their central executive powers have been enhanced; within each of them modern administrative routines have been elaborated and tightened up.

As each of these domains becomes enlarged and centralized, the consequences of its activities become greater, and its traffic with the others increases. The decisions of a handful of corporations bear upon military and political as well as upon economic developments around the world. The decisions of the military establishment rest upon and grievously affect political life as well as the very level of economic activity. The decisions made within the political domain determine economic activities and military programs. There is no longer, on the one hand, an economy, and, on the other hand, a political order containing a military establishment unimportant to politics and to money-making. There is a political economy linked, in a thousand ways, with military institutions and decisions. On each side of the world-split running through central Europe and around the Asiatic rimlands, there is an ever-increasing interlocking of economic, military, and political structures.[2] If there is government intervention in the corporate economy, so is there corporate intervention in the governmental process. In the structural sense, this triangle of power is the source of the interlocking directorate that is most important for the historical structure of the present.

The fact of the interlocking is clearly revealed at each of the points of crisis of modern capitalist society—slump, war, and boom. In each, men of decision are led to an awareness of the interdependence of the major institutional orders. In the nineteenth century, when the scale of all institutions was smaller, their liberal integration was achieved in the automatic economy, by an autonomous play of market forces, and in the automatic political domain, by the bargain and the vote. It was then assumed that out of the imbalance and friction that followed the limited decisions then possible a new equilibrium would in due course emerge. That can no longer be assumed, and it is not assumed by the men at the top of each of the three dominant hierarchies.

For given the scope of their consequences, decisions—and indecisions—in any one of these ramify into the others, and hence top decisions tend either to become co-ordinated or to lead to a commanding indecision. It has not always been like this. When numerous small entrepreneurs made up the economy, for example, many of them could fail and the consequences still remain local; political and military authorities did not intervene. But now, given political expectations and military commitments, can they afford to allow key units of the private corporate economy to break down in slump? Increasingly, they do intervene in economic affairs, and as they do so, the controlling decisions in each order are inspected by agents of the other two, and economic, military, and political structures are interlocked.

At the pinnacle of each of the three enlarged and centralized domains, there have arisen those higher circles which make up the economic, the political, and the military elites. At the top of the economy, among the corporate rich, there are the chief executives; at the top of the political order, the members of the political directorate; at the top of the military establishment, the elite of soldier-statesmen clustered in and around the Joint Chiefs of Staff and the upper echelon. As each of these domains has coincided with the others, as decisions tend to become total in their consequence, the leading men in each of the three domains of power—the warlords, the corporation chieftains, the political directorate—tend to come together, to form the power elite of America.

2

The higher circles in and around these command posts are often thought of in terms of what their members possess: they have a greater share than other people of the things and experiences that are most highly valued. From this

[2] Cf. Hans Gerth and C. Wright Mills, *Character and Social Structure* (New York: Harcourt, Brace, 1953), pp. 457ff.

point of view, the elite are simply those who have the most of what there is to have, which is generally held to include money, power, and prestige—as well as all the ways of life to which these lead.[3] But the elite are not simply those who have the most, for they could not 'have the most' were it not for their positions in the great institutions. For such institutions are the necessary bases of power, of wealth, and of prestige, and at the same time, the chief means of exercising power, of acquiring and retaining wealth, and of cashing in the higher claims for prestige.

By the powerful we mean, of course, those who are able to realize their will, even if others resist it. No one, accordingly, can be truly powerful unless he has access to the command of major institutions, for it is over these institutional means of power that the truly powerful are, in the first instance, powerful. Higher politicians and key officials of government command such institutional power; so do admirals and generals, and so do the major owners and executives of the larger corporations. Not all power, it is true, is anchored in and exercised by means of such institutions, but only within and through them can power be more or less continuous and important.

Wealth also is acquired and held in and through institutions. The pyramid of wealth cannot be understood merely in terms of the very rich; for the great inheriting families, as we shall see; are now supplemented by the corporate institutions of modern society: every one of the very rich families has been and is closely connected—always legally and frequently managerially as well—with one of the multi-million dollar corporations.

The modern corporation is the prime source of wealth, but, in latter-day capitalism, the political apparatus also opens and closes many avenues to wealth. The amount as well as the source of income, the power over consumer's goods as well as over productive capital, are determined by position within the political economy. If our interest in the very rich goes beyond their lavish or their miserly consumption, we must examine their relations to modern forms of corporate property as well as to the state; for such relations now determine the chances of men to secure big property and to receive high income.

Great prestige increasingly follows the major institutional units of the social structure. It is obvious that prestige depends, often quite decisively, upon access

---

[3] The statistical idea of choosing some value and calling those who have the most of it an elite derives, in modern times, from the Italian economist, Pareto, who puts the central point in this way: 'Let us assume that in every branch of human activity each individual is given an index which stands as a sign of his capacity, very much the way grades are given in the various subjects in examinations in school. The highest type of lawyer, for instance, will be given 10. The man who does not get a client will be given 1—reserving zero for the man who is an out-and-out idiot. To the man who has made his millions—honestly or dishonestly as the case may be—we will give 10. To the man who has earned his thousands we will give 6; to such as just manage to keep out of the poor-house, 1, keeping zero for those who get in. . . . So let us make a class of people who have the highest indices in their branch of activity, and to that class give the name of *elite*. Vilfredo Pareto, *The Mind and Society* (New York: Harcourt, Brace, 1935), par. 2027 and 2031. Those who follow this approach end up not with one elite, but with a number corresponding to the number of values they select. Like many rather abstract ways of reasoning, this one is useful because it forces us to think in a clear-cut way. For a skillful use of this approach, see the work of Harold D. Lasswell, in particular, *Politics: Who Gets What, When, How* (New York: McGraw-Hill, 1936); and for a more systematic use, H.D. Lasswell and Abraham Kaplan, *Power and Society* (New Haven: Yale University Press, 1950).

to the publicity machines that are now a central and normal feature of all the big institutions of modern America. Moreover, one feature of these hierarchies of corporation, state, and military establishment is that their top positions are increasingly interchangeable. One result of this is the accumulative nature of prestige. Claims for prestige, for example, may be initially based on military roles, then expressed in and augmented by an educational institution run by corporate executives, and cashed in, finally, in the political order, where, for General Eisenhower and those he represents, power and prestige finally meet at the very peak. Like wealth and power, prestige tends to be cumulative: the more of it you have, the more you can get. These values also tend to be translatable into one another: the wealthy find it easier than the poor to gain power; those with status find it easier than those without it to control opportunities for wealth.

If we took the one hundred most powerful men in America, the one hundred wealthiest, and the one hundred most celebrated away from the institutional positions they now occupy, away from their resources of men and women and money, away from the media of mass communication that are now focused upon them—then they would be powerless and poor and uncelebrated. For power is not of a man. Wealth does not center in the person of the wealthy. Celebrity is not inherent in any personality. To be celebrated, to be wealthy, to have power requires access to major institutions, for the institutional positions men occupy determine in large part their chances to have and to hold these valued experiences.

3

The people of the higher circles may also be conceived as members of a top social stratum, as a set of groups whose members know one another, see one another socially and at business, and so, in making decisions, take one another into account. The elite, according to this conception, feel themselves to be, and are felt by others to be, the inner circle of 'the upper social classes.'[4] They form a more or less compact social and psychological entity; they have become self-conscious members of a social class. People are either accepted into this class or they are not, and there is a qualitative split, rather than merely a numerical scale, separating them from those who are not elite. They are more or less aware of themselves as a social class and they behave toward one another differently from the way they do toward members of other classes. They accept one

[4] The conception of the elite as members of a top social stratum, is, of course, in line with the prevailing common-sense view of stratification. Technically, it is closer to 'status group' than to 'class,' and has been very well stated by Joseph A. Schumpeter, 'Social Classes in an Ethically Homogeneous Environment,' *Imperialism and Social Classes* (New York: Augustus M. Kelley, Inc., 1951), pp. 133ff., especially pp. 137–47. Cf. also his *Capitalism, Socialism and Democracy*, 3rd ed. (New York: Harper, 1950), Part II. For the distinction between class and status groups, see *From Max Weber: Essays in Sociology* (trans and ed. By Gerth and Mills; New York: Oxford University Press, 1946). For an analysis of Pareto's conception of the elite compared with Marx's conception of classes, as well as data on France, see Raymond Aron, 'Social Structures and Ruling Class,' *British Journal of Sociology*, vol. I, nos. 1 and 2 (1950).

another, understand one another, marry one another, tend to work and to think if not together at least alike.

Now, we do not want by our definition to prejudge whether the elite of the command posts are conscious members of such a socially recognized class, or whether considerable proportions of the elite derive from such a clear and distinct class. These are matters to be investigated. Yet in order to be able to recognize what we intend to investigate, we must note something that all biographies and memoirs of the wealthy and the powerful and the eminent make clear: no matter what else they may be, the people of these higher circles are involved in a set of overlapping 'crowds' and intricately connected 'cliques.' There is a kind of mutual attraction among those who 'sit on the same terrace'—although this often becomes clear to them, as well as to others, only at the point at which they feel the need to draw the line; only when, in their common defense, they come to understand what they have in common, and so close their ranks against outsiders.

The idea of such ruling stratum implies that most of its members have similar social origins, that throughout their lives they maintain a network of informal connections, and that to some degree there is an interchangeability of position between the various hierarchies of money and power and celebrity. We must, of course, note at once that if such an elite stratum does exist, its social visibility and its form, for very solid historical reasons, are quite different from those of the noble cousinhoods that once ruled various European nations.

That American society has never passed through a feudal epoch is of decisive importance to the nature of the American elite, as well as to American society as a historic whole. For it means that no nobility or aristocracy, established before the capitalist era, has stood in tense opposition to the higher bourgeoisie. It means that this bourgeoisie has monopolized not only wealth but prestige and power as well. It means that no set of noble families has commanded the top positions and monopolized the values that are generally held in high esteem; and certainly that no set has done so explicitly by inherited right. It means that no high church dignitaries or court nobilities, no entrenched landlords with honorific accouterments, no monopolist of high army posts have opposed the enriched bourgeoisie and in the name of birth and prerogative successfully resisted its self-making.

But this does *not* mean that there are no upper strata in the United States. That they emerged from a 'middle class' that had no recognized aristocratic superiors does not mean they remained middle class when enormous increases in wealth made their own superiority possible. Their origins and their newness may have made the upper strata less visible in America than elsewhere. But in America today there are in fact tiers and ranges of wealth and power of which people in the middle and lower ranks know very little and may not even dream. There are families who, in their well-being, are quite insulated from the economic jolts and lurches felt by the merely prosperous and those farther down the scale. There are also men of power who in quite small groups make decisions of enormous consequence for the underlying population.

The American elite entered modern history as a virtually unopposed bourgeoisie. No national bourgeoisie, before or since, has had such opportunities and advantages. Having no military neighbors, they easily occupied an isolated continent stocked with natural resources and immensely inviting to a willing labor force. A framework of power and an ideology for its justification were already at hand. Against mercantilist restriction, they inherited the principle of *laissez-faire;* against Southern planters, they imposed the principle of industrialism. The Revolutionary War put an end to colonial pretensions to nobility, as loyalists fled the country and many estates were broken up. The Jacksonian upheaval with its status revolution put an end to pretensions to monopoly of descent by the old New England families. The Civil War broke the power, and so in due course the prestige, of the ante-bellum South's claimants for the higher esteem. The tempo of the whole capitalist development made it impossible for an inherited nobility to develop and endure in America.

No fixed ruling class, anchored in agrarian life and coming to flower in military glory, could contain in America the historic thrust of commerce and industry, or subordinate to itself the capitalist elite—as capitalists were subordinated, for example, in Germany and Japan. Nor could such a ruling class anywhere in the world contain that of the United States when industrialized violence came to decide history. Witness the fate of Germany and Japan in the two world wars of the twentieth century; and indeed the fate of Britain herself and her model ruling class, as New York became the inevitable economic, and Washington the inevitable political capital of the western capitalist world. . . .

ACKNOWLEDGMENTS

Chapter 1: "The Promise", from SOCIOLOGICAL IMAGINATION by C. Wright Mills, copyright © 1959, 2000 by Oxford University Press, Inc. Used by permission of Oxford University Press, Inc.

Chapter 2: From AN INVITATION TO SOCIOLOGY by Peter L. Berger, copyright © 1963 by Peter L. Berger. Used by permission of Doubleday, a division of Random House, Inc.

Chapter 3: From THE SOCIAL CONSTRUCTION OF REALITY by Peter L. Berger and Thomas Luckmann, copyright © 1966 by Peter L. Berger and Thomas Luckmann. Used by permission of Doubleday, a division of Random House, Inc.

Chapter 4: From *Manifest of the Communist Party, Part I,* by Karl Marx and Friedrich Engels.

Chapter 5: Weber, Max, PROTESTANT ETHIC AND THE SPIRIT OF CAPITALISM, 1st Edition, © 1958. Reprinted by permission of Pearson Education, Inc., Upper Saddle River, NJ.

Chapter 6: From *The Division of Labor in Society* by Emile Durkheim. Copyright © 1933, the Macmillan Co.

Chapter 7: From *The Souls of Black Folk* by W. E. B. Du Bois (New York: Penguin, 1982; orig. 1903), pp. 43–53.

Chapter 8: From *Society in America* by Harriet Martineau. Copyright © 1962 by Seymour Martin Lipset. Used by permission of Doubleday, a division of Doubleday, New York.

Chapter 9: "If Men Were Seeking the Franchise" by Jane Addams. Reprinted courtesy of *Ladies Home Journal*. Copyright © 1913 by The Curtis Publishing Company.

Chapter 10: Reprinted with the permission of The Free Press, a Division of Simon & Schuster Adult Publishing Group, from SOCIAL THEORY AND SOCIAL STRUCTURE by Robert K. Merton. Copyright © 1967, 1968 by Robert K. Merton. All rights reserved.

Chapter 11: From *Mind, Self and Society: From the Standpoint of a Social Behaviorist* by George Herbert Mead (Chicago: University of Chicago Press, 1934), pp 140–164. Copyright © 1934 by the University of Chicago Press. Reprinted with permission of the University of Chicago Press.

Chapter 12: From THE PRESENTATION OF SELF IN EVERYDAY LIFE by Erving Goffman, copyright © 1959 by Erving Goffman. Used by permission of Doubleday, a division of Random House, Inc.

Chapter 13: "Body Ritual among the Nacirema" by Horace Miner. Reprinted courtesy of the American Anthropological Association from *American Anthropologist*, vol. 58, no.3, June, 1956.

Chapter 14: From *The Future of Marriage* by Jessie Bernard. Copyright © 1972 by Jessie Bernard. Used by permission of Yale University Press.

Chapter 15: From THE POWER ELITE, NEW EDITION by C. Wright Mills, copyright © 1956, 2000 by Oxford University Press, Inc. Used by permission of Oxford University Press, Inc.